THE UNOFFICIAL TALE OF Beauty and the Beast

BY EDWARD GROSS

All correspondence: 5715 N. Balsam, Las Vegas, NV 89130.

Distributed to the book trade by Publishers Group West. Distributed to the specialty trade by regional distributors.

First printing, Second Edition: December
Printed in the United States of America

9 8 7 6 5 4 3 2 1

To my son Teddy,...
for my wife and I,
ONCE UPON A TIME is indeed now...

CONTENTS

An Introduction...

In this time of inane television sitcoms, and detective shows which are more concerned with whether or not the leads will consummate their relationship than with detecting, it's refreshing to discover that true romance has returned to the air in the form of CBS' **Beauty and the Beast**.

This series, currently in the midst of its second season, took the viewing audience by surprise last year when it's tale of attorney Catherine Chandler and Vincent, the lion-like inhabitant of New York's Underground, touched the hearts of millions. The premise seemed a bit removed from what people, including those at the network, had expected, and yet the passion as displayed by actors Linda Hamilton and Ron Perlman in the title roles has ignited the imagination of the show's fans, and resulted in a cult following that other genre series have literally spent years attempting to develop, with very few actually achieving this highly coveted goal.

The Unofficial Tale of Beauty and the Beast serves as an indepth guide to the first season of the series, providing a behind the scenes look at the formation of the show itself, as well as a complete guide to the first year's episodes. Combination of story reviews and interviews with some of the people who have labored to bring these adventures to the television screen serve to bring the series alive for the reader.

This volume was put together with a lot of love for the efforts of creator Ron Koslow, cast members Hamilton and Perlman, as well as the many writers and directors who worked on it. It is the author's intent that through these pages, you the reader will experience at least some of the magic that is **Beauty and the Beast**.

—Edward Gross

BACK GROUND

Throughout its relatively short history, network television has been unable to truly support a weekly science fiction or fantasy series. This has been proven time and time again, and continues to be true to this day.

Despite what today's audience may think, such cult favorites as Rod Serling's **The Twilight Zone** and Gene Roddenberry's **Star Trek** were *not* tremendously successful, with the two of them constantly struggling just to stay on the air (although **Trek** had a somewhat tougher time than **TZ**). Since that time we've seen numerous series come and go with hardly a Neilson ripple, such as **Logan's Run**, **Fantastic Journey**, **Planet of the Apes**, **Battlestar Galactica**, **Buck Rogers**, **Phoenix**, **V** and **Starman**. This list will undoubtedly be followed by NBC's **Something is Out There**, which has performed terribly in its first several outings. Indeed, the only recent genre successes have been **Star Trek: The Next Generation**, **War of the Worlds** and **The** (new) **Twilight Zone**. Unfortunately, these shows have had their success in first-run syndication, where the ratings sweepstakes aren't quite as tough.

There have been two network genre shows which have proved themselves to be winners, one of which (**Alf**) will not be discussed in these pages. The other will. Naturally we're talking about CBS' **Beauty and the Beast**, which is now in the midst of its second season on the air, and continuing to woo the audience. But what's the secret of the show's success? *That* is a key question, and one which does not seem likely to be answered, because if it was answerable, you can be sure that there would have been numerous clones by the time of this writing (November, 1988).

The series is unique in its approach and appeal, and it hardly seems likely that someone could take these precise elements, mix them up exactly the same way and come up with the success that creator/supervising producer Ron Koslow has, aided, in no small part, by Linda Hamilton and Ron Perlman,the actors who have brought the title roles to life.

Like the majority of fairy tales, the original story of **Beauty and the Beast** was rather simplistic on a surface level, essentially reinforcing the adage that you can't judge a book by its cover. To wit, we have a princess who falls in love with a lion-man, a mutant to be sure, and yet a being who possesses more humanity than any man she has ever met. Their love is an unrequited one, until the moment when beauty kisses the beast, effectively transforming him into a prince, and allowing them to live happily ever after. Nice and simple, right? And yet it is a timeless story, filled with romance and hope for all of us, thus part of the reason for the success of the television series of the same name.

As a press release for the show states, "The original fable is part of a cycle of transformation myths, including such classics as **The Frog Prince**, in which the 'ugly being,' when accepted and shown love, is transformed into something beautiful. These myths are meant to instruct our culture on the transforming powers of love and the wisdom of prizing inner beauty and truth."

The tale of **Beauty and the Beast** was put on film in the classic Jean Cocteau film of the same name and, more recently, in a Cannon Film adaptation starring Rebecca DeMorney and John Savage. Both versions were period pieces, in true fairy tale settings, and it wasn't until Koslow studied the idea that its basic principles were applied to a modern setting.

"What we've tried to do is create a compelling, contemporary version of the original story, centering on a new mythic figure—an interesting kind of urban hero," Koslow recently explained. "We also wanted to tell a classical love story in a contemporary context. **Beauty and the Beast** affords us the opportunity to do just that, given the insurmountable obstacles which stand in the way of a complete relationship between Vincent and Catherine. We now have a chance to explore this kind of romance on television, with all its impossibility and longing."

The premise of the series is unique: Hamilton portrays attorney Catherine Chandler who, because of a case of mistaken identity, is attacked by a group of punks who slash up her face and leave her for dead in Central Park. Her body is found by Vincent, the Beast, who takes her beneath the streets of New York to a wondrous Underworld beyond imagination which is led by a man known only as Father, and populated by people who have migrated from the surface. There she heals, her face wrapped up in bandages and her only solace coming from the soothing voice of Vincent. The healing process is slow, and the two of them gradually fall in love. Then Catherine removes the bandages and discovers what Vincent truly is. Yet as was the case with her predecessors involved in this tale, her love remains, albeit in an unconsummated form.

"The relationship between Catherine and Vincent will be continually challenged by the fact that Vincent will remain who he is—a perfect man—ironically, Catherine's perfect soulmate—trapped in an imperfect body. The power of his character lies in the fact that he's a survivor who accepts who he is, and continues to move forward."

"This show really has a kind of romance, and it harkened back to a sort of former age," relates Howard Gordon, story editor of the show. "It just [appeals] on a real visceral level, the fact that there was this really deep romance, and he was this creature who was a hero for our time. A new hero, basically. The tone of the show is really two-tier. We really wanted to portray the above world as realistically as possible. Even if almost stylized, we wanted to emphasize the grittiness, speed and fast pace, in counterpoint to the real lyrical, soft-toned underworld. So in a broad thematic level, that's what we're trying to do. We're making every effort to keep this show unique. We don't want it to be 'Starsky and the Beast.' "

The modern setting of the series, particularly the Underground world, was inspired, according to Koslow, by an article he had read several years ago which described people who were living in the steam tunnels below the Waldorf Astoria in Manhattan, who were getting their food from the dumpsters behind the hotel restaurant, and generally living off that which was disposed of in the world above them. Further research revealed to the writer/producer that there were more than three hundred miles of tunnels beneath the city. The original purpose of these tunnels was to serve as conduits for steam, water and electricity, but the majority of these, built over a century ago, remain unexplored because the maps which hold the key to their locations have been long lost. There are also, as he discovered, underground caverns and rivers beneath Manhattan Island. All of this together inspired the world of Vincent and the others who live underground.

"Since then," Koslow said, "I have wanted to do a show which could incorporate the various textures of New York City, from the upper east side to the halls of power, the public institutions, and finally, this whole subterranean secret world below the streets."

The final ingredient of the **Beauty and the Beast** television series that separates it from all other incarnations of the fable, is that Catherine's job as a lawyer involves her in different situations on the surface, which manage to become intertwined with Vincent's. In addition, as the first season developed, the stories began to alternate between those having to do with people on the surface, and those who reside in the Underworld.

Director Paul Lynch, who has helmed numerous episodes of many genre shows, including **Star Trek: The Next Generation** and **The New Twilight Zone** as well as **Beauty and the Beast**, expresses the enthusiasm he felt for the series even *before* it ever went on the air. Interestingly, much of what he says held true throughout the first season.

"It's quite interesting and I think it's going to work," he said. "It's a family oriented show so there isn't a lot of violence. It's mostly human drama storytelling, and that's what I'm hoping will hold it together, because they are good human stories. One that I did was about old folks being evicted from their apartments, and how wrong that is. They seem to all be strong scripts, which was the same with **The Twilight Zone**. Do you remember **Eastside/Westside**? It was with George C. Scott as a welfare worker in New York City, and the stories are very similiar to the ones they did back then. They're not black and white stories, but they're stories about people with problems in today's world, and the DA gets involved in trying to solve the situation, and to help finish solving it is Perlman as Vincent. Let's hope it works. If you have a good script you're ninety five percent there.

"It's difficult," Lynch elaborated, "because of the way that television has changed over the years. Up until the late 1960's television was, for the most part, very intelligent, along the lines of **Playhouse 90**, **Climax** and so on. Good dramatic stories, and that's all they had. As the medium broadened its base, it sort of got away from serious television and I think it's been going that way ever since. I think **Beauty and the Beast** is the kind of show that can at least help to reverse that trend."

As the first season unfolded, the audience was exposed to a wide spectrum of stories, exploring the worlds of both Catherine and Vincent, while continually developing the relationship between the two. As Gordon notes, "The key word is romance. Every week should always try to push forth the story of Vincent and Catherine, and how these people deal with their impossible love."

For the most part, the episodes aired during the first season were far more effective than one might have believed possible at the beginning. The premise just didn't seem to lend itself to a continuing series, but those laboring in front of and behind the scenes have proved themselves beyond a doubt, and they have been well rewarded for their efforts. **Beauty and the Beast** is a solid ratings winner, and has developed the kind of cult following most shows can only dream of. Vincent, in particular, has ignited the imagination of the audience, much as the character of Mr. Spock did in the original **Star Trek**, and the romance between Beauty and the Beast has drawn a large female viewership, which would seem capable of keeping the show on the air for at least several seasons.

The Unofficial Tale of Beauty and the Beast is an in-depth look at the first season of this unique television experience, providing interviews with some of the people involved, and a guide to every episode aired, looking at the ingredients that have helped make this show the sensation it has become.

As they say in the promos, "Once upon a time is now...."

BIOGRAPHIES

LINDA HAMILTON:

CATHERINE CHANDLER

While genre fans are probably most familiar with actress Linda Hamilton for her roles in such films as **The Terminator**, **Children of the Corn** and **King Kong Lives**, she has made quite an impression in her role as attorney Catherine Chandler in **Beauty and the Beast**.

Hamilton was born and raised in Salisbury, on the Maryland Eastern Shore, where she lived until she went off to college. Her interest in acting began while still a child, when she began working with children's theatre groups. Subsequent to high school, she attended Washington College for two years, before moving to New York City, where she continued to expand her acting horizons by attending workshops at the Lee Strasberg Theatre Institute. Her student production credits include **Richard III** and **A View From the Bridge**. This was followed by her first professional appearance, on the daytime soap opera **Search for Tomorrow**.

In 1979, with Hollywood as her next career objective, she moved to the West Coast and starred in CBS' **Rape and Marriage: The Rideout Case** and **Country Gold**. Additional feature credits include **T.A.G.—The Assassination Game** and **Black Moon Rising**. Most recently, during the hiatus between **Beauty and the Beast**'s first and second season, she starred in CBS' highly acclaimed **Go Toward the Light**.

Hamilton has constantly proved what a diversified actress she really is, and it is this ability that she brings to the role of Catherine Chandler, resulting in the completely believable relationship which has developed between Beauty and the Beast.

RON PERLMAN:

VINCENT

Make-up to help bring a character to life is nothing new to actor Ron Perlman, but it is the role of the Beast in ***Beauty and the Beast*** *which, as he has admitted himself, has given him the greatest opportunity to practice his skills. Ironically, despite pounds of make-up applied to his face and body, Perlman is better able to eloquently express emotion than the majority of prime time television stars.*

To be transformed into Vincent, Perlman spends the early hours of each shooting day in the make-up artist's chair. As already noted, this is nothing new to him, as witnessed by such films as ***Quest for Fire*** *and* ***Name of the Rose****. In the former he spent approximately eight months running around bare-foot and nearly naked in the frozen bogs of Scotland playing a pre-historic Ulam tribesman, a characterization which required a great deal of make-up. For the latter, which co-starred him with Academy Award winner Sean Connery and F. Murray Abraham, he portrayed the facially deformed, hunchbacked monk, Salvatore.*

"I have the least known face of anyone in the business," Perlman recently explained, "and it looks like that will continue into the foreseeable future."

The son of a jazz drummer, Perlman was born in Manhattan, and began his career in high school, appearing on stage first as a comedian and then as an actor. Attending the City University of New York he continued his appearances in theatre productions, and then earned a Master of Fine Arts degree at the university of Minnesota. Upon returning to New York, he joined the Classic Stage Company, spending two years performing in the works of such writers as Shakespeare, Chekhov, O'Neill, Ibsen and Pinter.

Eventually he was cast in the role of the Emperor in the highly successful, four-hour Off-Broadway play, ***The Architect and the Emperor of Assyria,*** *which was destined to tour Europe. He also starred on Broadway in* ***American Heroes*** *and in various productions of* ***The Resistable Rise of Arturo Ui, Pal Joey, Tartuffe, Measure for Measure, House of the Blue Leaves, Two Gentlemen of Verona*** *and* ***The Iceman Cometh.*** *Speaking of "ice," he starred in the feature film* ***Ice Pirates*** *and at Lincoln Center in* ***La Tragedie De Carmen.***

Naturally Perlman will have a diversified career in the future, but as Vincent he has struck a chord with the public, touching their hearts and igniting their imagination.

ROY DOTRICE: FATHER

One of **Beauty and the Beast**'s greatest strengths lies in its wonderful supporting cast, who add believability to the storylines, and help create the worlds represented by New York City, and the realm which lies beneath it. And the finest supporting actor among them is undoubtedly Roy Dotrice.

He stars as Father, leader of the Underworld and the closest thing to a parent that Vincent has ever known. As we would eventually learn, Father had once resided above ground, but was conspired against and blacklisted in the 1950's. Since then, he has made his world beneath the streets of the city.

A native of England, acting had never occurred to Dotrice until, at the age of sixteen, he was captured by the Germans during World War II. He was a Prisoner of War for three and a half years, and during that time actually acted in plays the German's had forced the prisoners to be in, beginning with the role of Mio in Maxwell Anderson's **Winterstet**. During his time as a prisoner, he continued to act and learn the game of baseball, as taught to him by his fellow American prisoners.

Between the years 1945 and 1958, he acted in and/or directed more than 500 repertory productions. A year later he joined the Royal Shakespeare Company where he performed with such artists as Sir Laurence Olivier, Charles Laughton, John Gielgud, Paul Scofield and Paul Robeson. His love of baseball, triggered by his capture by the Germans, inspired him to put together a team made up of his fellow actors.

Dotrice spent eight years playing lead roles in both Stratford and London, and then went on to appear in numerous plays on Broadway, including a one-man show called **Brief Lives**, which ran for 1700 performances. He also received a Tony Award nomination for his acclaimed work in **A Life**.

He has appeared in more than a dozen films, including a stint as Leopold Mozart in **Amadeus**. Television credits include the one-man productions of **Mister Lincoln** and **Dickens of London**, as well as such episodic work as **The Wizard, Magnum P.I., Remington**

Steele, The A-Team and **Hart to Hart.**

His television movies include **Family Reunion** and **The Caretaker**. In addition, 1968 saw him voted Television Actor of the Year for his work in **Brief Lives**.

It is hoped that his role of Father will continue to evolve during the second season of **Beauty and the Beast**, giving this fine actor the opportunity to provide further layers to his characterization.

JAY ACOVONE:
JOE MAXWELL

*In **Beauty and the Beast**, actor Jay Acovone portrays Deputy District Attorney Joe Maxwell, Catherine Chandler's immediate supervisor and the man who often-times unwittingly sets up the adventure which will involve Catherine and Vincent.*

*Born in Mahopac, New York, Acovone began perusing the acting bug in local theatre, and continued his studies at the American Academy of Dramatic Arts and the Lee Strasberg Theatre Institute. While in New York, he eventually got the opportunity to portray recurring characters in the soap operas **As the World Turns** and **Search for Tomorrow**.*

*In 1985, Acovone moved to Los Angeles after being cast as Jack Rado in the Spelling/Kramer production **Hollywood Beat**. Subsequent to that, he has appeared in such episodic series as **Matlock**, **Werewolf** and **Down and Out in Beverly Hills**.*

*More recently on television, he portrayed Quartermaster Maselli in Dan Curtis' $100 million production of **War and Remembrance**. His feature film credits include **Cruising**, which co-starred Al Pacino, **Cold Steel** and the forthcoming **976-Evil**, which was directed by **Nightmare on Elm Street**'s Robert Englund.*

REN WOODS:
EDIE

After her harrowing accident at the hands of punks, Catherine Chandler desperately needed friends. One of the first she acquired was Edie, portrayed by actress Ren Woods, a sharp and streetwise computer whiz who works in the New York District Attorney office with her.

Born in Chicago and raised in Portland, Oregon, Woods got her first taste of performing at age 9 when she joined "The Three Little Souls," a successful rhythm and blues singing group. When the destined-to-be actress was twelve, the group relocated to California where exposure on **Soul**, the first black television special, led to an invitation from Bob Hope to join him in entertaining the troops in Vietnam. At fourteen, she and the group opened for Sammy Davis, Jr. at Carnegie Hall.

When the group finally disbanded, Woods remained in California and won the starring role of Dorothy in the Los Angeles company production of **The Wiz**, which was followed by a co-starring role in the Richard Pryor film **Car Wash**. More recently she appeared in **Brother**

From Another Planet and **Jumpin' Jack Flash**, with her next role being in the political adventure **Walker**.

Her television credits include **Roots, Hill Street Blues** and **The Jeffersons**.

An accomplished vocalist, Woods has released a pair of solo albums.

PAUL JUNGER WITT & TONY THOMAS: EXECUTIVE PRODUCERS

Paul Junger Witt and Tony Thomas have created quite a track record together. Under the Witt/Thomas/Harris [as in Susan Harris], they serve as co-executive producers of the Emmy Award-winning comedy series ***Golden Girls****, and served in the same positions on such previous series as* ***Soap, Benson, It Takes Two, Hail to the Chief*** *and* ***I'm a Big Girl Now****. They are also executive producers of the syndicated* ***It's a Living****, which has the distinction of being the first primetime series to go from network telecast to off-network syndication. Since then it has been followed by such series as* ***Charles in Charge, The New Twilight Zone*** *and* ***The Days and Nights of Molly Dodd****.*

Prior to Witt/Thomas/Harris, they collaborated, as a part of Danny Thomas Productions, on such series as ***Fay*** *and* ***The Practice*** *and such television movies as* ***Satan's Triangle, Griffin and Phoenix*** *and* ***Bloodsport****. Other TV movies include* ***Cold Night's Death, No Place to Run, The Letters*** *and the highly acclaimed* ***Brian's Song****.*

Beauty and the Beast *marks their first foray in to the science fiction/fantasy genre, and judging by their success, one can only hope that they will explore it further in the future.*

RON KOSLOW: CREATOR/SUPERVISING PRODUCER

Amazingly, **Beauty and the Beast** is creator/supervising producer Ron Koslow's first foray into episodic television, and yet it has turned into a success which must be beyond even his wildest expectations.

Born in Denver, Colorado, Koslow spent the early portion of his life in St. Louis and moved to Los Angeles when he was ten years old. Eventually he attended the University of California at Berkley and the UCLA film school, and became a member of the California Bar after earning a law degree at Loyola University.

While still attending college, Koslow sold his first screenplay, **Lifeguard**. Later he would write and produce such films as **Firstborn** and **Into the Night**. His TV movie credits are **Lady of the House** and **Swan Song**. Judging by his fertile imagination which has resulted in the creation of **Beauty and the Beast**, one can only wait with anticipation to see what he turns his creative sights to next.

FIRST SEASON

Episode One

"Beauty and the Beast"

Written by Ron Koslow

Directed by Richard Franklin

"It's a forgotten place, but it's warm and it's safe, and we have all the room that we need. So we live here and live as well as we can, and we try to take care of each other. It's our city, down here."

—Vincent

We begin with a shot of a tree, and the peaceful sound of a bird singing. The words "Once Upon a Time" flash on the screen. We pull back to see the bustle of Manhattan, with the words "..in the city of New York" superimposed.

This immediately sets the tone for the episode and the ensuing series, effectively stating that we are about to experience a classic fairy tale juxtaposed on a modern setting.

As we are introduced to Catherine Chandler, we learn that she is the daughter of a corporate lawyer and is following in her father's footsteps, which is a fact she's not necessarily happy about. She wants more out of life, but doesn't know what will fulfill her needs.

That evening she attends a party where she tries to console an old friend whose life is hitting rock bottom. In the midst of this conversation, we meet her boyfriend, who turns out to be a chauvinistic jerk. Angry, Catherine departs and tries hailing a cab, but with little success. A stranger comes up to her, offering to hail one. Suddenly a van pulls up, she is thrown inside, referred to as Carol and told by one of the several men inside that she "has got to learn to keep her mouth shut." She unsuccessfully tries to tell them that she's not Carol. One of the men pulls out a knife, tells her again that she's got to stop talking to people and adds, "You're going to remember, every time you look in the mirror."

The van drives through Central Park, dumps her body on the grass and continues without even slowing down. Later, a cloaked figure approaches her unconscious body, lifts it up in his arms and begins to carry her away through various tunnels and down a spiral staircase that seems to go on forever.

Eventually Catherine awakens, her head, with the exception of her mouth, completely wrapped in bandages. She hears a male's voice (Vincent), who tells her that she's okay and that she's in a place of safety. Catherine is obviously disoriented. Vincent explains that "my father and I" treated her injuries, which include a broken rib.

Vincent moves into the outer room, where Father is awaiting him, immediately asking how he could bring a stranger to their home. Vincent points out that there was no choice. Although we still haven't seen Vincent's face yet, Father says, "Do you know what they'd do to you if they caught you? They'd kill you, or put you behind bars and you'd wish you were dead." This does not affect Vincent at all. He says that there is no way he could have turned his back on her. Father reluctantly accepts this, but tells Vincent that as soon as she's well, Catherine must leave, and he must not tell her "anything."

Catherine awakens later and is fed soup by Vincent. She wants to know where she is, but he states that that must remain secret. She pleads, promising that she would keep his secret. Catherine also makes note of a tapping on pipes which never stops. He explains that it is merely the sound of people "talking" to each other.

While this is going on, director Richard Franklin is repeating something he had done to great success in his feature film, **Psycho II**. In that film, he panned the bedroom of Norman Bates, giving the audience a great deal of insight to the character by revealing the child's room he still slept in. Here it works to as good effect, as we see relics from the world above, spanning some thirty years. We see everything from old editions of Shakespeare to a small diner-table juke box. In effect, we're seeing the romanticism of literature of the past, coupled with evidence from the world above.

Catherine continues to beg him to tell her where they are, and he finally does, stating that they are below the city in a world of tunnels and chambers which society has forgotten about. As the conversation continues, Vincent explains that he was abandoned as a child, found by the man who would eventually become his Father and named him Vincent, after the hospital he was found in front of. Catherine doesn't know what to believe. Vincent brings another spoonful of soup to her mouth and we see, for the first time, his furred hand. She touches it, and pulls back with a gasp.

Back on the surface, Catherine's father is furious that the police have leaked the story of his daughter's disappearance. The lieutenant says that it's impossible to keep the disappearance of a socialite secret, adding that there is no sign of her, although the search will continue.

Underground Catherine tries to make her way around the room she's in, blindly stumbling into things. Vincent is watching from outside the room. Catherine turns around and tells him to come in, having felt his presence. He offers to continue reading **Great Expectations** to her, but she says that it won't help. Catherine admits that she's frightened. He understands, pointing out that her strength is coming back and she will be ready to leave soon. In the meantime, he's going to get her some tea to soothe her nerves.

Vincent goes off to have one of the child-helpers get the tea from Chinatown—as the *entire* city is connected via these tunnels. Still in the room, Catherine desperately starts unwrapping the bandages which cover her head. She finds a mirror and is horrified to see the scars which have resulted from the slashing she underwent. Suddenly Vincent steps out from behind her, and she sees his face in the mirror. Catherine screams and shrinks away, frightened by his lion-like appearance. Dejected, Vincent backs away as well, leaving the room. Needless to say, Catherine is stunned. Collapsing to the bed, she begins to weep.

"I've never regretted what I am," Vincent says with anguish upon returning, "until now."

This whole scene is brilliantly handled—and will be further expanded upon in the Richard Franklin interview—creating a terrific sense of suspense and mystery. Our first visual introduction to Vincent is a bit startling, equaling the impact of the "reveals" from **Twilight Zone**'s "Eye of the Beholder" and the Lon Chaney version of **Phantom of the Opera**, which is precisely what Franklin intended. Yet as startling as Vincent's appearance is, the soothing tones of his voice we've heard throughout the episode help to belie his looks. Catherine reacts as only a human would, and Vincent's responding sadness is truly touching.

Catherine wants to know how this could have happened to him, but Vincent says he isn't sure. The facts are simple: he was born, and he survived. He adds that the time has come for her to go back home. Catherine begs him to tell her that this whole thing is a nightmare; that it didn't actually happen to her. Naturally Vincent can't do that. Putting it succinctly, he says: "Catherine, you survived, and what you endured will make you stronger." She doesn't believe that she has his kind of strength, but he insists that she does. In this conversation, we can sense the true depth of love that has developed between them. Both of them have been changed, probably forever. Vincent leads Catherine out of the tunnels, and enroute she sees samples of some of the people who reside there. As Vincent said, this is truly a world of wonder.

Before Catherine leaves, she declares that his secret is safe with her, which he says he knows, and which he knew from the moment she first began trusting him. Finally they part, a parting which is extremely painful for both of them, particularly Vincent. This was the first woman he has given his heart to, and now it feels as though that heart is breaking.

Later, Catherine is in the hospital for plastic surgery. Knocked out for surgery, she dreams of being in her father's office building, her face still scarred, facing all the people who work there, who start to actually *laugh* at her. She is feeling lost and lonely, when, finally, she sees the reassuring face of Vincent, whose mere presence actually puts her at peace.

She awakens again in a hospital bed, her face wrapped in bandages just as was the case earlier. A doctor enters the room, telling her that "it's over." Was this all a dream? Was Vincent merely a figment of her imagination? Has she been here all the time? The doctor says that if there's anything he can do, she shouldn't hesitate to ask. And with that he's gone without another word. Catherine, who thinks he's still there, softly whispers that he can read her the last chapter of **Great Expectations**. Naturally there is no response.

Elsewhere in the city at that exact moment, Vincent is climbing a building and rests on a ledge, staring into the city at night.

These two moments provide an interesting contrast. On the one hand we've got Catherine yearning for the kind of companionship that Vincent provided while she was recuperating, and yet she is left coldly alone by the doctor who sees her as nothing more than another patient. On the other, we've got Vincent, staring at the city in awe, desperately wishing he were a part of it. Together, we sense the loneliness of these two individuals who are perfect for each other, and yet are kept apart by their physical differences. We can *feel* their loneliness, and can't help but be reminded of a time in our own lives when we wanted to reach out to *someone* to help us through the pain.

Eight months later, Catherine is looking fine and goes to the DA's office for a job. Joe Maxwell is hesitant to hire her, believing that she's just some "rich guy's girl," but the DA tells her to hire her, throw everything that he can at her and see how she handles it. Ultimately Joe agrees. Continuing to put her life together, she goes to the gymnasium of Isaac Stubbs, who she's paying to teach her self-defense so that what had happened to her before will never happen again. As Isaac explains it, he teaches New York City street fighting: whatever it takes to come out alive.

Back at the DA's office, Catherine asks Edie for some help on something, but the woman gives her a hard time, stating that Catherine is one of those people who sheds a few tears for humanity to ease her conscience and then goes back to her penthouse. Catherine smiles, saying that the description just isn't true. Not believing her, Edie punches up information on her, and is startled to see a photograph of Catherine's scarred face. She's instantly apologetic, but Catherine tells her not to worry about it.

In the Underground, Vincent is bemoaning Catherine's departure, saying that she's still a part of him. Father responds that she can only bring him unhappiness. "Then I'll be unhappy," Vincent snaps. "I can feel what she's feeling, I know what she's thinking. When she's frightened. Or happy. Or sad."

Father advises him not to let his act of kindness destroy him. Perhaps, Vincent argues, he has no choice.

Catherine, working with Edie, is trying to determine if the woman she was mistaken for was ever found by the punks who slashed her face. After some checking, the computer gives them the address of the right Carol, and she goes to her apartment. The woman is hesitant to talk to her, even after Catherine shows her the scars on her cheek. Speaking through the door, Catherine says that if Carol ever needs someone to talk to, she can call. Her card is slipped under the door.

Back in Isaac's gym, Catherine is being held tightly by the man, who tells her that she had better do something to defend herself. In response, she bites his arm, stomps on his foot, flips him over, kicks his gut and actually threatens him with a baseball bat. Isaac, delighted by her progress, halts her. "Is that you?" he demands. They share a laugh.

Going back home, Catherine starts to do some work, when she gets the feeling that someone is out on her terrace. Pulling a gun from the bureau drawer, she steps outside to see Vincent. They embrace each other, and express their happiness at seeing each other. She invites him inside, and he's immediately sorry that he came to see her. She, on the other hand, is glad that he did. She tells him that she's going to be strong. He knows this, and tries to explain that he feels the things that she does. "Your pain is my pain," he says simply. "It's almost as though we were one." Vincent goes on to say that he wanted to see her one last time. Catherine is stunned. Does this mean they're never going to see each other again. Vincent explains that he has seen her world, and there is no place in it for him.

This and what follows in the conversation are really quite touching. Once again, the audience can truly feel the anguish that these two people are feeling at being together, and yet being kept apart by circumstances beyond their control. Even if they're apart, their love—despite the harsh realities of the world—will go on.

When Catherine goes to work the next morning, she is surprised to find Carol waiting for her. Apparently she's been plagued with guilt at what those men did to Catherine. Carol goes on to explain that she had been working for an escort service run by one Marty Belmont who used the service to threaten his customers, and he would use the girls to help bribe them. She refused to go along with this plan, and Belmont grew concerned that she would go straight to the police. The men that attacked were Belmont's men. Carol says that she would be willing to testify. Delighted, Catherine arranges for warrants. She wants to put Carol up in a friend's apartment, and tells her to phone once she gets there. Unfortunately, as Carol leaves the DA's office, she is followed.

Catherine comes by later after picking up some groceries. She climbs the stairs, calling out to Carol, and is horrified to find the woman's lifeless body sprawled out on the floor. Two of Belmont's men step out of the shadows, making it quite clear that their intention is to kill her too. Using everything that Isaac taught her, Catherine picks up a lamp, rushes them and runs down the stairs, only to run up against two more henchmen. She goes back up into an empty room. While this is happening, Vincent, in the Underground, has sensed the danger she's in. He starts running out of the tunnel to her aid. Back in the building, the men are searching for her.

Vincent is riding atop a subway car, speeding his efforts to reach Catherine in time.

After continuing their search, the men finally locate Catherine and raise a gun to her head. The trigger is about to be pulled when a howling Vincent bursts through the wall and attacks the men, clawing and killing them. Then he senses Catherine's eyes upon him, and there is a wonderful moment where the camera closes in on Vincent's eyes, which suddenly soften as they glance at Catherine. The Emperor is suddenly naked. Brilliant touch.

The police are carting the bodies away, with the Lieutenant we had met earlier wondering what in God's name had happened here. One thing he's certain of: he's going to find out. Thankfully this potential subplot of the lone cop trying to hunt down the creature [ala **The Incredible**

Hulk] was dropped immediately after the pilot.

Elsewhere, Vincent and Catherine have gone off to be alone. Catherine says that she owes him everything, but he dismisses the statement. He is a part of her, just as she is a part of him. "Wherever I am, I'm with you," he says sincerely. They embrace, and go their own separate ways...for now.

The pilot for **Beauty and the Beast** was perhaps one of the best to come along in quite some time, somehow managing to make the somewhat intangible fantasy genre palatable for the general television audience. The characters are completely identifiable, their situations realistic and their adventures completely involving.

"The only reason I'm here is that I felt **Beauty and the Beast** could be something different," creator/supervising producer Ron Koslow recently explained. "I wasn't interested in doing the business as usual type of thing for television. The consensus was that this show could be the doorway to exploring certain aspects of relationships that hadn't been explored on television for quite a while. We wanted to create a love story in the grand old tradition of lovers kept apart. I think a great, almost insurmountable obstacle allows everything to get a lot more passionate and more powerful. Certainly in terms of contemporary love stories, there really isn't anything keeping people apart. In our story, we have a twist of fate which has locked a perfect man inside this beast's body."

The making of the pilot for the series is a fascinating tale unto itself, and a much more detailed accounting of it can be found in the ensuing interview with director Richard Franklin.

AN INTERVIEW WITH DIRECTOR RICHARD FRANKLIN

Hollywood continues to search for a new master of suspense to assume the mantle from the late Alfred Hitchcock. For a time, it seemed as though Brian De Palma would fit the bill, but his thrillers, as effective as they are, have gone beyond mere homage and into an area where they sometimes lift whole sequences or plot devices from Hitchcock's work.

Australian-born Richard Franklin, on the other hand, emerged as a filmmaker shortly before Hitchcock's death, and some say he's rapidly shaping into the Master's most likely successor. His credits include the Jamie Lee Curtis vehicle ***Road Games****, the excellent* ***Psycho II****, the kids-and-espionage yarn* ***Cloak and Dagger*** *and the "anthropological thriller,"* ***Link****. Last year, he directed the pilot episode of CBS'* ***Beauty and the Beast****, which helped to launch the highly successful series of the same name.*

Franklin was born in Melbourne, Australia, and attended school there. At age 10 he gained his first 8MM camera, and immediately began spending his every spare moment making films.

In 1967, he began attending USC, where his classmates included George Lucas, John Carpenter and John Milius. While at school, he arranged a three-week retrospective of Alfred Hitchcock's films, and through this, first met the Master.

"I had to write a letter to request permission to screen ***Rope****," Franklin says. "One morning, I was called to the Dean's office to take a phone call. The voice on the other end of the line was unmistakable. He said, 'Good morning, Mr. Franklin.' As a nineteen-year-old kid, I was terrified. But I must have had a bit of courage, because I said, 'We would love to have you come down and talk to the students.' He agreed, and I shared a stage with my idol, chairing the discussion of his films."*

Returning to Australia in 1969, Franklin directed TV cop shows, short films and documentaries before making his motion picture directorial debut on the unsuccessful ***True Story of Eskimo Nell****. He followed with the highly acclaimed* ***Patrick****, a supernatural thriller which owed more than a passing nod to Hitchcock. From there, he followed through with the aforementioned films, carving himself a niche in the thriller genre.*

The following interview with Franklin chronicles his involvement with ***Beauty and the Beast****, a credit he is particularly proud of—and justifiably so—as well as the current environment working in the science fiction/fantasy genre.*

Q:

How did your involvement with **Beauty and the Beast** come about?

A:

I got a call from my agent and he said, "There's a script here for a pilot that might interest you." It was by Ron Koslow, and I knew Ron's work from **Into the Night**. Indeed, I had read a straighter draft of the script than the one John Landis ended up filming, which I appeared in. I thought, "Well, this should be interesting," because Ron's a good writer. So I read it and liked the script very much. I have been a fan of the original Cocteau film for quite some time, needless to say. I wasn't quite sure what we were going to do or how it was going to work in a modern context, but I thought, "Why not?" I came over and did it. It's not a terribly exciting story [laughs], but that's how it came about. It's the way most things happen, other than a project which you initiate yourself, like **Link**, which took six years to get made. The nice thing about television is that it happens quickly. It's not a situation where in six months, *if* the right elements come together we *might* make this. It's kind of like, "Can you come to New York on Thursday," and that's literally what I did. I left the Australian summer and my next memory was climbing along some girders on the Manhattan Bridge, which was a location we were going to film, but ended up not doing so. Anyway, it was quite peculiar, but I've always wanted to film in New York and this gave me the opportunity.

Q:

What is it about New York that you found so attractive?

A:

It's just a city that I find attractive. Do I have to tell a New Yorker? I've been getting to New York as often as I can on my sort of yo-yo life over the Pacific the last fifteen years. I've been buying round trip tickets to New York as often as I could, trying to spend a week there while a script was being read or I wanted to get someone interested in a project. I just find it an exciting place and I wanted to film there.

Q:

You have no aversion going from films to television?

A:

The first thing, I suppose, you have to understand is that most Australian directors, because our industry has been small or nonexistent prior to the early seventies, all crossed over and still do. Peter Weir still does commercials on occasion, as I do.

Q:

You do?

A:

Oh sure. Not here, but in Australia. I'm not saying that I wouldn't do them here, but I haven't. Funnily enough, people don't really make that crossover here, although, point two is the fact that recently—it would appear, and I can't corroborate this except to say that there's been articles about it in **American Film** and other places—there have been a number of feature directors who have done, specifically, television pilots. From my point of view, it provided some sort of income regulation, because of residuals and additional payments if the show gets picked up and it goes for a second season and so on. It's attractive in that way. The other thing that's particularly attractive is that it's quick. You can spend twelve to eighteen months or longer on a feature and then, as is the case with **Link**, have the frustration of seeing it disappear in a matter of days. It just doesn't warrant that amount of time. Admittedly in theory a television show airs only once. I know that's not really true, but in theory you're just going for one hour as opposed to even one week. That somehow seemed more worthwhile to me, because it has all the same creative rewards, and it's wonderfully quick. **Link** had been such a slow experience on so many levels, and I'm a director who likes to work fast, on the set in particular. I thought it would be a challenge to do television. I started in television, of course, directing a couple of years worth of a show in Australia during the early seventies before I did my first feature.

There were many attractions. New York, television, money and, probably most of all, the actual material, which I found interesting because like most things that attract me, it was in that grey area where one's first reaction might be to say, "Boy, this thing really might not work," which is the reaction when you look at **Beauty and the Beast** as a television show. One's immediate response is to say, "That sounds iffy." Well, that's always what attracts me creatively. Projects that are on that tightrope between being magical and mundane, and I try to keep it as much on the magical side as I can.

Q:

It's really quite wonderful, and I hope the series can live up to what you achieved in the pilot.

A:

I have no way of answering that. The difficulty I think they're going to have is that **Beauty and the Beast** is a fantasy that sustains through to a transformation, that is the Beast turning into a Prince. Now the longer the show goes on, the longer they're holding back on that transformation. I'm not saying that there are any plans to *ever* have him transforming into a prince, but there is a big payoff in the original film and story, which is that he turns into a prince so that everything turns out happily. The difficulty in doing the show week after week is that he can't turn into a prince at the end, so the stories are always kind of open-ended and the relationship between Beauty and the Beast is not moving towards a conclusion in the same way that it does in the original.

But the interesting thing about the pilot, I discovered, as opposed to a movie, is you're trying to lay out things open-ended because you're trying to whet the appetite of the audience for things to come, so it's an interesting form, because you keep coming up with conflicts and complexities which you then don't resolve, which is fun in a pilot but it may get hard to sustain.

Q:

What do you think it's got going for it that might make it a success?

A:

I think its unique tonality, that is it's a fantasy, and quite a romantic one...if I say old fashioned, I don't mean fifties or sixties. What I mean is Victorian. It's a fantasy of literature of a hundred years ago. It has a type of romanticism that I think is unique. I don't know where else on television I see such things. I think the most interesting thing in it is the relationship between Beauty and the Beast. And to me, what's also interesting is this other world, this fantasy underworld if you like, which, as opposed to the alligators of the New York sewer system image, is an image of an almost Medieval kingdom under the streets of New York. It is highly fanciful, but I think extremely interesting and appealing. To me, that setting will sustain much interest, and the fact that that setting is juxtaposed with New York. It's like the antithesis of New York, and I think that's interesting. Without in anyway belittling Linda's performance, because I think she's a very interesting character and a wonderful actress, Ron Perlman in that astonishing Rick Baker make-up is one of the most charismatic things that I've ever seen. I don't know how else to describe him. He's one of the most appealing people imaginable. It was very funny, actually, because I got so used to seeing him in his make-up that when on occasion he would arrive or leave the set without the make-up, I would kind of shrink back in the way that people would to the Beast, because I got so used to seeing him as the beast, and he looked so splendid. Anyway, that's kind of a list of about five things that I think are appealing about the show. You can sort them out under headings if you like [laughs]. I kind of went from one thing to another. I started with tonality and ended up with make-up.

What appeals (to an audience) is what usually appeals to me. Something on that dangerous sort of tightrope between something magical and mundane. My favorite things are things that you think about after you've seen them, and they've worked wonderfully. You think back and say, "My God, that really could have been nothing." What was magical *could* have been nothing.

Q:

Your trademark of suspense still came through in the show. I even felt suspense when Linda Hamilton began to slowly remove the bandages from her head.

A:

That sort of came with the script. I won't say that I was consciously working to build suspense. It's something that I do without a great deal of effort. I had some fun with the scene where she was abducted in the beginning, although that was more of an action scene, where the van drives across the screen from right to left, and when it's gone, she's gone. That's the equivalent of someone saying, "One minute I was walking down the street, and the next minute I was hit over the head." You don't see the person coming who hits you. Or something like a shark attack. That's what I tried to go for there, and I would have loved to have done that scene for cinema. When the guys rough her up in the van, and we had this metallic rubber floor put in the van so that I could really make it look like these guys were rough-housing her around, but the van is actually like a gym mat. That was probably a subtlety that goes by pretty quickly on a television screen. That scene was fun. The final set piece, in the dark house, was a contrivance to build a bit of suspense. I tried to make more of her coming up the stairs with the sound of the television in the distance, although in television you have to move along so much quicker. Suspense, by its nature, consists of moments of waiting for things to happen, but you tend to play suspense a little less on television and go for action. But, conversely, in cinema, we probably would have had difficulty showing in cuts the Beast getting all the way across town to save her, whereas because of the television or commercial-like nature of television, we could make that conceit and get him across town in the time it took her to get down a flight of stairs [laughs].

I think what interested me most, other than what attracted me, was the challenge. I had to do several dialogue scenes, eight from memory, in which we did not see the Beast as was the case with the shark in the first **Jaws**, because that was something we were holding back on; in which we could not see the girl's face because her face was "damaged." Well, I looked at the old **Twilight Zone** with Donna Douglas, "Eye of the Beholder," and I looked at how it was done in that. It was done quite simply, just with camera moves and so on, and I did it with slightly more complicated camera moves. That was slightly unusual for television to shoot, in some cases, four or five page dialogue scenes in one shot. On television that's not often done. Unlike in a movie, where you don't have to reach a finite running time, a one hour television show has to hit the running time within a second. There has to be an exact length that relates to commercial time and so on. I can't remember exactly what it is, but there's no leeway in that, so the more scenes you shoot in one shot, the less flexibility you've got if you mistime the length of the scene. That approach was, I think, very unusual for television, but it was dictated not by the desire to do clever things with the camera (for example, there's a 360 in one scene), but because I couldn't show either the face of Beauty or the face of the Beast. From memory, there were eight scenes, and from each scene I worked out a little scenario. I showed just a little more of the Beast. One moment we saw just the cloak, then we'd see what color his hair was, eventually we would see his hand, which I think was the first ad-break, and then I was quite pleased with the moment when she touches his hand and he recoils. I thought the moment worked real well. The moment at which the Beast first appears, I really took directly from the Lon Chaney **Phantom of the Opera**.

I had every intention of doing all sorts of fancy cuts and opticals with a shot of her looking at her own face in the mirror, and then suddenly he appears in the mirror and she turns around. I had quite an elaborate scenario worked out, but then I looked at the simplicity of that appearance in **Phantom of the Opera**, and I realized that for whatever reason, that moment is one of the great reveals of all time, and it's really just done in a cut. I didn't even do a cut. From memory, I just had Ron stand behind Linda, and at the moment she pulls the mirror down and we see her face for the first time without the bandages, I had him step up from behind her. He doesn't even come through the door. He sort of seems to come from her body. Intellectually, that might sound interesting, but it was immensely simple and was based on the idea that we would be looking at the scars on her face in the way that one can't resist looking at car accidents and such things, as much as one doesn't want to. Then suddenly he would be there, and to me Rick Baker's make-up was so incredible, that I didn't want to gild the lily.

Having seen the make-up, I decided that I wasn't going to turn this into a big, fancy cutting sequence. I would just let him step forward into the light and let the make-up do its job. So quite a bit of thought went into that, and it could have been a lot more elaborate. It could have been played as much more of a shock moment, but it seemed to me that it wasn't entirely valid for the Beast to be shocking.

Q:

In the past, you and I have discussed the art of subtlety, how the more subtle it is, the more effective it often is.

A:

That was a moment that might be of interest to your readers. Particularly because they compare that moment to the one in the original **Phantom**.

Q:

An interesting scene is when the guys are approaching her, she screams and Vincent's head pops up, and the whole intercutting with him getting to her in time.

A:

I think he actually turns his head. That was a good moment. As I say, the whole scene is a real conceit because he couldn't possible get across town in that time. He couldn't get on the train, let alone get to her. That sort of takes the conceit of a contracted television format as per commercials, and uses it to our advantage. As I say, in cinema we would have had to have her trapped in the house a lot longer, just to justify his getting that distance. But in the shorter format on television, it was possible to bring him there almost in a montage. Yeah, that was kind of fun. I liked it, too, and it had a sort of strange heroic quality, like the cavalry was coming to the rescue.

Q:

He takes care of the guys, then he notices Linda Hamilton staring at him and his eyes soften, the roaring stops. Beautiful moment.

A:

I would have liked to have played with that moment more, but there's the feeling in television that you have to get to your climax and get out quickly. I would like to have made more of it. He knows that she perceives him as an animal at that moment, and he feels remorse and guilt. I would love to have played more with that, but it's not the nature of the medium. I thought it was an important moment when she sees his animal side.

Q:

He's naked in front of her for the first time, so to speak.

A:

Yeah, and then we hear the sirens coming and she almost has to save him. If one played more with that moment, the idea would be that he would feel such guilt that he would surrender himself to the police because he feels like he's behaved as an animal. But she saves him.

Q:

Was the cast in place before you got there?

A:

No. Ron Perlman had been selected, and I couldn't have been more delighted, but Linda came in literally at the eleventh hour. I was astonished, actually, that someone of her caliber would do this. Because they effectively sign on for about five years when they do a series. Having seen her in **The Terminator**, I was just knocked out at having someone like that playing the girl. I guess she had her personal reasons for wanting to go back into television at this moment, and I think we were all lucky. Roy Dotrice, who plays Vincent's father, was someone that I was delighted to have an opportunity to work with. He's just one of the most amazing character actors...well, actors, to be honest. Character actors sound like they always play the same character. In fact, he always plays completely different characters. I don't say that most people would instantly realize that this was the father in **Amadeus**, for example. He has the most astonishing range as an actor. He's played Lincoln on Broadway, and lots of Shakespeare in England, and it was a thrill to work with someone that good. I remember when we did the scene in which he tells Vincent that he has to forget the girl. It was very late at night, and we'd been waiting around all day to do the scene. It was like the last day of shooting in LA, and we had to finish this. From memory, Roy had been waiting for many hours and when we finished he asked me if I wanted to see it another way. I thought it was perfect the way it was, and couldn't be improved, and he said, "Let me show you another way." He did it a second time, and did it just as well, but in an entirely different way. I can't remember which one we ended up using, but they were both equally good. A guy that good doesn't need direction, and to do that after that many hours of waiting around, I was just blown away. But take a look at his credits, and you'll see that he's an amazing actor. I guess he has two or three scenes in the pilot, but he's a recurring character.

They were a pleasure to work with. It was fun working with John McMartin, who played her father, because I'm a big Stephen Salkind fan, and he was the original Ben in the original **Follies**, so it was exciting to work with him.

Q:

Would you say you brought anything to the pilot that would help define what the series would be?

A:

I don't know, because I don't know which way the series has gone. That would probably be a better question to ask Ron Koslow. All I can say is that I think I set the tone for the piece.

That's probably the thing I think about most. Once I know what the tone is, that is to what degree it's realistic, what degree it's fantasy, to what degree we're having fun with it, to what degree we're making fun of it, to what degree we're taking it seriously, to what degree it's romantic...I mean, all of those shadings are what concerns me in the first instance. Given that I am attracted to material that is hard to pull off, hard to make convincing, getting the tone right is immensely important to me. If we'd gone a bit too realistic or a bit too fairy tale, the whole thing could have collapsed. I think in that area I probably have dictated the direction they have to go. There's no question, also, that the first director who works with the actors on their characters, tends to define the way that the characters go. At least I imagine so. The other directors are probably cursing me now, because the actors have such a clear idea of what they want to do, and it comes from the evolution of the character which I was fortunate enough to be there for and a party to. I would say in those two areas, tone and character, the one person who I think should be mentioned, apart from Rick Baker who is a genius and deserves his reputation, is Roy Wagner, the director of photography, who had just come off of **Nightmare on Elm Street 3**. Roy had just shot that, and I had been wanting to work with him for years. He had shot some film with a colleague of mine from film school, and I had admired his style for a long time. I think's he's the modern Stanley Cortes. The look of the show has so much to do with the lighting. I was able to stage things in a particular way, because he's one of the first cameramen I've ever worked with to who if I ever said, "Now, it will be black over there"...that is, if I stand the Beast in the corner, he will be in the darkness. With Roy I was always assured that that was the case. Cameramen are often tempted to put lights on for the sake of lighting, because they figure that's what they're doing. It's like asking a painter to leave a piece of the canvas blank if you ask them to leave part of the set dark. A lesser cameraman would have put the lights on, and I would have had to do it with the cutting. Because of the way he lit those sets, particularly the underground, I was able to stage scenes in a much more interesting way, because I could rely on him to keep the Beast in shadow. Very often there's not much logic to that. Where, for example, you want there to be light on the girl's face but not light on the Beast's face. It is not logical from the point of view of the physics of lighting, but it is emotionally apt that the Beast be a dark figure and the girl be a light figure. Well, more than emotionally. Obviously, it's symbolic. A lot of cameramen would be emphatic and say that I can't stand them next to each other and have one of them in light and the other in darkness. But Roy, who is a great cameraman, was not only willing to do that, but *able* to do that. I'm not sure how many modern cameramen could light in that style.

Q:

That underground set was incredible.

A:

He's really a great cameraman, and when you ask me to what extent I dictated where the show went, I believe he had every bit as much to do with it. In fact, the first five or six episodes of the show were also shot by him. They asked him to stay on just to keep that look going into the series itself. He has not done episodic TV before, so it was a major step for him to turn down features and do more episodes. But he did because he cared enough about the show.

Q:

It's great when you have that much enthusiasm from the crew.

A:

Philosophically, I'm very much like Andy Warhol. I believe that what we consider to be artistically important and what is really of cultural significance are entirely different things. I'm talking about the Campbell's Soup can painting. What we consider to be lofty and what really is meaningful, are two quite different things. I'm not saying that I'm necessarily a pop artist, but I'm saying it's possible to say something as meaningful in a television commercial, given the time restrictions and the fact you're trying to sell something, as it is in a feature film. There's no difference. I think one should not take an elitist approach to art and culture. That's my qualification. But for a feature cameraman to do television is a dubious career move, and Roy did that because, just as I wanted to work with him, he wanted to work with me. He's a great cameraman, and I think anyone looking at that show will see a style of lighting that just has not ever been seen on television, other than in old movies that are shown on television.

Q:

In your estimation, what can an audience expect from **Beauty and the Beast**?

A:

That's an awfully hard question. I think they can expect to be surprised. I'm not saying that that's what I set out to do, but I was surprised when I read the script, you were surprised when you saw the pilot...everyone seems to react that way. I don't know why, because I don't know too many people who don't like the Jean Cocteau film. I think they thought that commercial television would not mesh with such fare, if you know what I mean. While I don't think we've achieved what Cocteau did, it was interesting. I was reading his diary while we were shooting, which dealt with the making of **Beauty and the Beast**. One thing that he said early on is that "fantasy is such a brittle thing," that he took the view that what he should do was approach the thing not as if he was making a magical jewel box, but as if he was making a table. Something functional and simple, straightforward and solid. That's the way I approached this, and I think even I was surprised by how those magical moments in a story that's lasted more than a hundred years kind of surfaced and were appealing. I think the other subplot, the sort of crime story that might superficially be significant, tended to become secondary to what was the secondary element. In fact, the element that I didn't even go for while I was directing, was the element of fantasy, of romance as in **Wuthering Heights**, the romance of the Victorian romantic novelists. Those secondary elements surfaced on their own, and surprised even me. I hoped that that's what would happen, and it did; and I have Cocteau to thank for it. It could have vanished. I think the audience could expect to be surprised.

What's more, and this goes back to your first question, is how the thing came about. I must say that I'm a little tired of the modern cinema, particularly where the fantasy-horror genre is concerned, and it's a genre I've concerned myself with. I'm tired of having to reduce all stories to the lowest common denominator of what will appeal to a twelve year old. And I'm afraid that is what one is continually forced to do when one works in this genre. I'm not saying that when you make **Plenty** or **Out of Africa** that you're not making a film for adults, but the minute you make fantasy for the modern cinema, you're thinking about what will scare twelve year olds. I have an eleven year old daughter, so I'm not putting them down, but what I'm saying is that some stories, and I think that **Beauty and the Beast** is one of them, do not necessarily come down easily to the level of a twelve year old. It was extremely refreshing, and a real paradox if you think about it, to be able to make this for adults.

Look at the demographics. The marketing experts tell you that when you're making cinema, particularly for this genre, that you're aiming at the young teenagers and up to twenty at the absolute outside. You look at the demographics of the television audience, and you're mostly aiming at families and/or married people with kids, in their late 20s through their 50s and 60s. It is possible, as paradoxical as it sounds, to actually be a little more adult in your sensibilities, and that, to me, was refreshing. I know that sounds like a paradox and quite unlike what one does in commercial television, but I have to tell you that in recent films I've made, there has been so much pressure to always think of the twelve year olds.

Q:

Is that a problem you had with **Link**?

A:

Oh yeah. It was refreshing to do something with the idea, "Gee, how will my mother react to this scene? How will my wife react?" I was thinking of adults, rather than thinking of kids.

Q:

When you did **Psycho II**, were you thinking of kids? That's *not* the impression I got.

A:

No, when I made **Psycho II**, I was thinking about doing almost a treatise to the original **Psycho**, because the original picture was twenty two years old. I tended to think of people going to the cinema twenty two years ago, which meant people who were at least in their thirties now. I was focusing primarily on people who knew **Psycho** well. I was taking the others into account, but I figured it would be better to go over the heads of the young kids. We gave them a few cheap thrills [laughs], but better to go over their heads than to insult the people who saw **Psycho** as some kind of intellectual, artistic work, which it really is. Perish the thought that I would ever say that I was thinking intellectually [laughs], but if the studio had thought about it, they would have wanted me to aim the thing at the twelve year old audience. I suspect that that sort of pressure was put on Tony on the third one. The feeling is that if you don't give them cheap thrills, the kids won't like it. Well on television you don't have that problem, because you're dealing with something that's censored already. I took **Beauty**'s opening scene in the van [where Catherine is attacked] further than it goes now. Not much farther, but I did something that was mildly perverse, which was that I had the guy who cuts her up lick the knife before doing so, and that was particularly eerie.

I won't say why. I think it's evident why it's eerie, and I couldn't see how that was censorable. But the producers felt that we shouldn't even try it on the television board. Someone licking a knife is not something you would censor. The guy who played the "carver" had the most wonderful sense of humor, and we had a lot of fun with this. We talked about what might motivate this character. I don't want to make too light of it, because there was an instance in which a New York model was slashed. But considering the sort of psychological reason that someone might do something like this, I thought it was appropriate for this guy to take some relish, and I thought it would be clearly odd. Certainly if he had hacked up the girl and *then* licked the blood off the blade, that would have been vile; the sort of thing that one might expect in the average movie for twelve year olds. But the idea that someone would kind of lick the blade to test how sharp it was, for example, to me was not unlike the blade through the hand type thing we did in **Psycho II**. To me it was kind of a horrific image that would then set up what was about to happen. It was a strong moment that I wish we had put in, because, as we discussed, what always interests me is not so much what is censorable, as what conveys an idea without being offensive. It seems that more often than not, people look for the pyrotechnics that will allow them to show the body imploding, exploding, being hacked apart or whatever.

Q:

Do you think that the studios are correct, that a filmmaker has to aim for the twelve year olds?

A:

Without opening a can of worms here, I think that there is a tendency among distributors in particular to underestimate their audiences. I could go further than that. I think sometimes there's a tendency among distributors to hold their audience in contempt. I suppose you can't blame them when you see the way some people behave in movie theatres, but I think it leads to a particularly low lowest common denominator being dictated to filmmakers by distributors. The idea is, "Listen, what they want is of the standard of the stuff we sell at the concession stand. They want popcorn and movies. They don't want filet steak." And it's often hard to convince them that you can give them filet steak often at the same price. They almost don't want to give them filet steak. I think it comes from underestimating the public, which I know is what P.T. Barnum said makes you rich.

Maybe I just came off a bad experience with Cannon on **Link**, but I think distributors en-masse tend to hold their audience in contempt, and I don't agree with that. I would rather over-estimate an audience's intelligence, which is basically what I did with **Psycho II**. I could not have pitched that at much more of an intellectual level than I did, to be honest, and we didn't lose money by overestimating the American public. The wonderful thing to me was watching that movie with a midnight audience in Times Square. You can imagine the kind of audience that was, but the astonishing thing was they were not experts on **Psycho** in the way you and I are, yet I swear to you that every subtlety in that movie communicated to that audience. I'm not saying that they could come out afterwards and discuss the light motifs in the way that we could, but it did not go over their heads. In other words, they conveyed, or communicated, on an emotional level, every nuance of that picture.

I am not of the P.T. Barnum school. I would rather go in the other direction. I don't know if you can, actually, because on that I agree with Frank Capra who said that even if individually the audience doesn't have the I.Q. that one might wish them to have, enmasse there's this peculiar thing where a group of people together seem to respond according to the highest intellectual level among them. The minute that one person picks up on something, it goes through the audience like a wave, and so a group of people has a higher I.Q. than any individual. That's not my idea, it's Frank Capra's, and I think it's absolutely true. Sure, there are certain instances where people respond like a mob, but when they're watching movies, they tend to be sophisticated and extremely intelligent. I don't like this notion that we've got to bring it down to the level of twelve year olds. It would be wonderful to say that a twelve year old has such an incredible inate sense of storytelling, that we should bring it *up* to a twelve year old level, but the word down is always used. The minute they say, "We're trying to appeal to the twelve year old," they add, "Let's bring it down to their level." That I don't like.

Fortunately, you don't have that on television, so that's yet another reason why I enjoyed doing **Beauty and the Beast**. It appeals to twelve year olds and adults alike, and is representative of the way working in the genre *should* be.

Episode Two

"Terrible Savior"

Written by George R.R. Martin

Directed by Alan Cooke

"I know your heart, Catherine. But sometimes the words that are not spoken are the truest words of all."

—Vincent

Several people are riding the New York City subway system. The train pulls into a stop, allowing one person to get off and two punks to get on. They immediately begin to start threatening the people, until all but an elderly woman leave the car. They approach her and demand her pocket book. When she resists they are about to punch her. Suddenly the door to the car swings open, and a cloaked figure—with lots of hair/fur—runs towards them. It raises a clawed hand and slashes one of the punks across the throat. It quickly dispatches the second one and leaves the car, leaving the grateful woman behind.

Next morning, the news is reporting their lead story on the "Subway Slasher." The DA's office says that they're working on the situation. Catherine is assigned the task of trying to find out what's going on. Joe Maxwell hands her photos of the two victims, noting that, "It looks like they went a couple of rounds with a tiger, only this tiger walks around on two feet and half the city thinks he's a hero."

Catherine studies the photos, and has a mental flashback to the conclusion of episode one where Vincent disposes of Marty Belmont's men in a savage manner. Could he be responsible for this act as well? The flashback ended, Joe says that the slasher can take care of himself, and hands her files on karate schools and the like, believing that that would be the best place for her to start.

Leaving her office, Catherine goes to Isaac's gym, and begins asking him about the Subway Slasher. The man is hesitant to respond, and she points out that whoever he is, he's killing people. "I notice you didn't say innocent people," replies Isaac. Catherine doesn't want to get involved in *that* particular discussion. When she wants to know who's side he's one, he responds that he'll show her.

Later, they move down the street and go to the karate training school of the Protectors, "ordinary people wanting to take care of each other." Jason Walker, the leader of these people, is introduced to Catherine. Jason believes that whoever saved the woman should get a commendation. The conversation that follows, continues down the usual "vigilante" path with Jason and Catherine essentially arguing both sides of the issue: that the courts is the only system they have or that the system doesn't work. They leave the gym, Catherine pondering one question in particular: could the slasher be Vincent? When she's alone, Catherine goes to a tunnel area, and begins tapping on a pipe, trying to contact Vincent. Unfortunately there is no response, and she departs.

That night, she is reading on her terrace and falls asleep. The wind blows strongly and she is suddenly awakened by Vincent's climbing up to see her. "You came," she says happily as she walks over and hugs him. He does not return the hug. Pulling back she looks into his face as he bares his fangs and moves in for an attack. Naturally, Catherine awakens from her nightmare. She is all alone.

Next morning she reports to work, and has Edie pull the file on the woman saved by the slasher. She goes to talk to her, but the woman is completely uncooperative, believing, like so many others, that the slasher is nothing short of being a hero. Catherine tries to appeal to her on a personal level, stating that "a friend" may have been personally involved. Finally the woman says that her savior didn't have hands—he had claws. And his face was not a human, but more like a "terrible angel" that came to save her.

This is an effective scene, quite reminiscent of the Charles Bronson film **Death Wish**, in which someone has been saved by the vigilante, and when that person is questioned by the police, he says he didn't see anything. This is all quite understandable. After all, why would someone want to betray the person who just saved their life?

Catherine finally goes to see Vincent to confront him with her fears. She's upset that he never came to see her. Vincent says he felt her pain, and still feels her fear. Does she want to know if he's the mysterious shadow? Must she hear the words before she trusts? If so, he states categorically that it is not him. He moves towards her and she shrinks away in fear. This tears at him. They talk a little longer, with Vincent uttering the words reprinted at the outset of this synopsis. Catherine, extremely saddened, goes back to the surface, with Vincent moving to a bridge area which is suspended over a seemingly bottomless pit.

The place where Vincent goes is fascinating in that it helps to paint a small part of the immenseness of the Underworld. There are endless caverns, tunnels and hidden areas, which combine to help reinforce the reality of this realm.

Father approaches Vincent, and they begin talking about Catherine. Father tries once again to convince Vincent that the world above is not the place for them, and that Catherine is irrevocably linked with that world. Vincent's sadness is tangible, and it's a credit to Ron Perlman that he so effectively conveys emotion from beneath his make-up.

That night Catherine has a dream which involves Vincent. Then, just before she awakens again, she has the image of Jason in Vincent's cloak. Next day she goes back to the office of the Protectors, and begins another conversation with Jason. The man says that everyone still needs their gods and heroes to look up to, and then he relates the tale of an IRT worker laying down some track, who saw a creature of some kind down in the tunnels. The street people speak of it also; a creature that haunts the dark places, with the face of a demon and the soul of an angel. "Inside we're all children, still afraid of the dark, wishing that there really was a Batman," explains Jason. Catherine doesn't necessarily agree with this. Once again the conversation moves to the point where they discuss the system, and the effectiveness of the rules that govern society. Catherine moves over to a weapons wall and studies the various items there, including Samurai swords, ninja stars and clawed gloves.

Going back to the DA's office, Catherine tells Joe Maxwell that they should make a move against Jason Walker. Joe says they're already investigating him, and that despite the fact he fits the bill, he has an alibi and has been under police surveillance since the investigation into the slasher began.

That night, on another subway, a punk starts to bother a woman. She tries to get up, he holds her down, is slapped and gets angry. He moves in for the attack. An elderly man warns him to let her go. The man goes off to get the police officer. The door opens and the cloaked figure enters, after knocking the old man aside. He attacks the punk and is halted by a cop. He claws the cop and actually leaps through a window of the subway car.

One of the Underworld's child helpers has seen the figure move into one of the tunnels, and then communicates the information to Father, who in turn contacts Vincent. The next day the news is reporting what happened, saying that the punk was killed and that a cop was critically injured. Vincent goes to see Catherine. She apologizes to him for the fear she demonstrated. Vincent understands, saying that he knows the vigilante went into one of the older tunnels. Catherine wants to know where so that she can tell the police, but Vincent fears that the investigation of one tunnel would lead to an investigation of all the tunnels. There must be another way. Then, Vincent begins to ponder his right to stop the vigilante. "Am I so very different?" he asks. Catherine says that he is.

Red, one of Jason's men, climbs down the fire escape of a building across from Catherine's, and through binoculars sees her talking to Vincent. Naturally he is stunned at seeing this legend brought to life.

The next day Edie puts Catherine in touch with some information on tunnels beneath an old hotel which is now the headquarters of the Protectors. Catherine investigates and learns of their location through old newspapers from the turn of the century. It's obvious that these tunnels have been long forgotten. She leaves the library, gets into a cab and is stunned to see that the driver is one of the Protectors who takes her to Jason. There, Jason explains that they discovered the tunnels quite accidentally. The "demon" brought to life is a symbol for the people, he feels. "The deaths weren't important," he says, "but the legend was." Catherine wants to know about the policeman who is still in critical condition. He says that people make mistakes, to which Catherine sarcastically responds that it's a shame, then, that his legend doesn't exist. Jason begs to differ, and wants to know everything about the *true* legend brought to life seen with her at home.

Underground, Vincent senses what Catherine is experiencing. Back at the Protectors' headquarters, Jason confronts her with the news of Red's spying on her. Jason says that he is a mirror image of the legend. Catherine wants to leave. Jason opens a secret panel and allows her entrance into one of the tunnels. Jason and two of his people begin escorting her through it. Jason leaves them alone for a moment. She tries to convince them that they have to talk Jason out of this madness. They do not respond. Then Jason, in cloak and costume, approaches them, demanding that Catherine tell him everything she knows about the creature. Threatened, she says that he told her no one would get hurt. "Jason would never hurt you," says the ominous voice, sounding more like Darth Vader than Jason Walker. On Catherine's stunned reaction we cut to Vincent running through the tunnels. Jason extends one of his clawed hands to aid in the extraction of information. Suddenly Vincent is there, growling. Seeing him, Jason runs, leaps over him and readies for combat. With one blow, Vincent sends Jason sprawling. He manages to get to his feet and starts running deeper into the tunnel. Vincent pursues him.

This whole set-up is very suspenseful, and it's interesting to see that Jason, once he puts on his costume, forgets that he is really a human being; believing, instead, that he is truly the legend that these people are looking up to. His threats to Catherine also serve as a succinct counter-point to his words to the effect that what he is doing is the best thing for society. Unless you have the nobility of someone like Vincent, or even a comic book hero like Superman, even the best of intentions are corruptible.

The chase eventually leads to the bridge area we had seen earlier, with both Jason and Vincent occupying opposite ends of it. They run towards each other. Jason slashes Vincent across the chest, while Vincent , angry, swings out at Jason , sending him flying. Vincent approaches Jason, and they ready to swing out at each other again. Suddenly one of the boards gives way, and Vincent falls through, just barely being able to get a hold which stops his plummeting into the abyss. Jason moves in for the kill, but suddenly stops himself, perhaps realizing what he's about to do; how he's about to go against everything that he has held dear. Instead, he grabs hold of a rope and starts to swing away to safety, but it snaps, sending him plummeting to his death.

Back at Catherine's penthouse, she and Vincent discuss Jason's death, adding that the legend he created will continue to live on.

"How can one man have so much courage, empathy and passion and so little mercy?" she asks.

"He found it," Vincent replies solemnly. "In the end."

While "Terrible Savior" may lack the passion of the pilot episode, it does effectively demonstrate how a continuing series of **Beauty and the Beast** will evolve, as well as the intertwining worlds of both Catherine and Vincent. The vigilante plot is, admittedly, old hat by this point, and yet in the hands of the cast and crew it seems to take on new vitality. Perhaps this is because of the characterizations of Catherine and Vincent, and the *truth* that Perlman and Hamilton bring to their roles. Director Alan Cooke handles things nicely, particularly the action sequences, which are extremely well coordinated. High praise indeed when considering that one battle takes place in a subway car, with the other on a narrow bridge.

Episode Three

"Siege"

Written by David Peckinpah

Directed by Paul Lynch

"It's all still very new. Sometimes I wonder how all those little pieces will ever fit together again."

—Catherine

An elderly man (Mr. Langer) is playing Billy Joel's "This Night Can Last Forever" on the piano. There is the sound of a car screeching to a halt outside. Suddenly flaming bottles of liquor are thrown through the basement window, where the man is. The two men responsible leave. Vincent leaps through the window and helps the man to safety, after beating out the flames with his cloak. Vincent refuses to step out of the shadows where the man, who is grateful to him, would be able to see him. We learn that he is one of several tenants who refuse to be driven out of their home by people who want the building empty for financial reasons.

This opening provides an interesting contrast. Langer's playing "This Night Can Last Forever," is suddenly the intended victim of a bombing, but he is rescued by Vincent. The question is whether or not the song is the plea for the lives of the people in the building to be left alone, or if it is a battlecry. A proclamation that they will not be driven from their homes. It's a question which will continue to be pursued as the episode unfolds.

Catherine attends a formal event, where she meets the extremely rich real estate magnate Elliot Birch, and is immediately taken by him. The two begin talking, and we see that the feeling is mutual. Meanwhile, Langer continues detailing the living situation with Vincent, who promises that *something* will be done. Back at the party, Catherine and Elliot continue to talk about their respective careers. The words of Elliot, surprisingly, mirror the tones and meaning of Vincent's, and this touches Catherine's heart. The image is reinforced as the two leave in a limousine, and Vincent, who is walking in the shadows, takes notice of them.

In a bar, the man behind the punks who tried to torch the building, explains that "something went wrong," but that he will continue the efforts. Meanwhile, Catherine bids Elliot a good night. He wants to know when he can see her again. She smiles and hands him her card, telling him to phone. When she is upstairs, she finds Vincent on her balcony. He is leaving her a message about the people in the building. She sees that he's hurt, and offers to get him some aid. "I'm not the one who needs your help, Catherine," he says, wanting to know if she can investigate and find out who is behind the threats. She'll do her best. Sensing what she's feeling regarding Elliot, Vincent suggests that she follow her heart. Certainly a noble enough sentiment, considering the pain he is starting to experience.

The next day, Catherine goes down to the building where she talks to Langer, who details what has been happening to them in this rent-controlled building. They approach a man who is allegedly in charge of the punks. He approaches the old man and says that he really ought to take their "generous offer" before the building is condemned or something worse happens. Catherine asks if he's threatening them, but the man replies that he's merely stating the way things are. Learning his name is Leo Munday, who works for the company that is trying to get its hands on the building, Catherine goes back to the DA's office. There she learns that Munday had been accused of strong-arm tactics in the past, but there have been no convictions. She asks Joe if they can move on him, but he says they have nothing to tie Munday in with the punks. She then asks if they have to wait until someone is killed before something is done? "We can't do the outraged 'the system stinks' act, because we're part of it," Joe counters. "You give me the tools, and I do a job on him." Going back to her desk, Catherine and Edie are talking about the situation, but they are interrupted by flowers from Elliot which have been placed on Catherine's desk. She asks Edie to gather whatever information she can regarding the company that is trying to purchase the building. Then the phone rings, and Elliot asks her for a dinner date, which grants.

Father and Vincent discuss the fact that Catherine is falling in love with someone else. Father suggests that he let it happen. "My mind tells me to rejoice for her, she deserves the happiness, but my heart is dying," says Vincent sincerely. "I'm poisoned by feelings I've never felt before." Father tries to console him, expressing that he has always dreaded the arrival of this moment, but, by the same token, he always felt that it would someday come. This relationship, between Vincent and Catherine, can never be. This does not lighten the burden at all.

Although this it quickly becomes a repetitive commentary on the show: this scene once again demonstrates the sheer believability that Ron Perlman conveys as Vincent. How many of us have been in love with someone, and then been pained when that someone began to fall in love with somebody else? How lost did we feel? Perlman conveys all of this and more.

Catherine and Elliot are walking through the streets, arm in arm, talking about the sheer magic of the city. Elsewhere, Langer and his wife are walking down the street when they are assaulted by a punk [incidentally, the word "punk" seems to sum up the common street people who pick on the defenseless, hence its use so often in these pages] who threatens them physically. Suddenly there is the sound of growling, and Vincent moves in to defend them, effortlessly dispatching him. The punk jumps into a waiting car, but has dropped his wallet, which Vincent picks up.

The punks meet up with Leo Munday and try to detail what happened. Munday is furious, calling them too stupid to do a simple job.

Catherine and Elliot embrace passionately. Vincent is a "witness" to this at the entrance to one of the tunnels. He feels what is happening, even though he is not actually there.

Getting a tip, Catherine calls Langer and tells him that they can bring in the men who threatened him and his wife. Seh needs to know if he will testify. The man responds in the affirmative. She's delighted, telling him that she'll call as soon as they get some news. Edie approaches and says that three buildings on that particular block are scheduled to be demolished. If the fourth one is also demolished, it would give the holding companies that own the other three the complete block. That event is only being held up because of the old people who refuse to move. Catherine believes that these holding companies are only a veil put up by someone who owns all of them. She needs to know who the person is.

Joe Maxwell puts in the order for the punks to be brought in. Catherine wants him to get them to strike a deal to testify against Munday. Maxwell, smiling, says that the possibility of such an action does exist. Catherine steps out of his office, and is surprised to find Elliot, who has brought lunch to her, because she was too busy to go out. She appreciates the offer, but says that she can't have a romantic lunch in her office. He good-naturedly leaves. She follows him into the hall and tells him that the gesture was not a complete waste, and he leaves with a dinner date for that evening.

Catherine leaves her office, drops a cryptic note off at a street-corner musician, and then escorts Langer and his wife to the DA office. Munday is in his car, observing everything. She walks over, informs him that two of his people are being held and that she will see that he is put away. As Catherine moves off, Munday is confident that "she has nothing."

That evening, Vincent greets Catherine at the threshold of a tunnel. Catherine believes that they are on the road to ending the violence against Langer and his friends. She apologizes to him about her relationship with Elliot.

"We both knew that the bond between us was only a dream," says Vincent. Catherine replies that their bond is the most real thing she has ever experienced, but when asked if she loves "this man," she says that she honestly doesn't know. He says that some day someone else will come, and she will live in another dream. Catherine says that she doesn't want to lose him, as Vincent disappears into the tunnel.

Munday, meanwhile, has seen Catherine come out of the tunnel. He approaches the entrance and is stunned to find Vincent's footprints. Munday informs his superior that Catherine could be trouble. He tells him not to worry about her, just complete his task: clear out that building. We discover that the man he's talking to is one of Elliot's right hand men.

At the DA's office, Edie provides her with information pertaining to the holding companies under investigation, including the fact that they all share the same law firm. Going there, she comes across the man, Mr. Arthur, who was talking to Munday. She hands him the names of the holding companies, explaining that she wants to contact the people in charge of them. He says that he can't help her with this because the names are privileged information. She comes right out and asks if the buildings are owned by Elliot Burch, but he refuses to reply. She leaves, and Arthur tells his secretary to get Elliot on the phone.

Catherine confronts Joe Maxwell with the fact that the punks are back on the streets because someone made bail. Catherine goes to Elliot's office, and confronts him with her knowledge that he owns the buildings on that block. Elliot claims he didn't know what was going on there, or of Munday's reputation. On the one hand he claims innocence, but on the other he says that even if thirty or fifty old people are moved, the project he has planned for that block will provide jobs for ten thousand, and millions of dollars for new jobs. "At what price?" she demands. "We're talking about human beings." She leaves the building, crying. Eventually she makes her way to Langer's apartment, who invites her in. Catherine explains that the punks are back on the streets, and that they must take every precaution they can. She is invited for dinner. Sophie, Langer's wife, tells Catherine that they must fight, because if they don't, the "madness will start again."

Munday and his men arrive at the building and shut down the power and telephone lines. Langer, Sophie and Catherine go to warn the others. The punks start making their way up the stairs, armed with baseball bats and other weapons. Their search continues, anger mounting as the intended victims are nowhere to be found. Vincent, meanwhile, senses the danger and starts running out of the tunnels. In a move which repeats, exactly, the one from the pilot, he rides the top of a subway to get there faster [aided in no small part by stock footage]. Munday approaches Catherine, who manages to defend herself quite nicely, particularly after Munday implies that he's going to rape her. Vincent leaps through a window and launches a vicious attack, killing all of the punks, except Munday who accidentally falls to his death. All of these people smile at him, and tell him to go before the police arrive. Some people want to know who he was, but Langer says, "It doesn't matter. He's a friend."

Elliot meets Catherine in front of her building, and she informs him that she has enough on him to stop his company. The building, quite frankly, she says, is going to stay exactly where it is, as will the people who live there.

On her terrace, Catherine picks up **The Sonnets of William Shakespeare**, which is inscribed by Vincent: “Shakespeare knew everything.” Pressed within the book is a rose. As she reads, she hears Vincent’s voice in her head, detailing a sonnet which perfectly fits him, and their relationship.

“Siege” once again gives us the delicate balance between romance and action adventure, and demonstrates how simple it would be to cross the fine line and turn it into something like **The Incredible Hulk**. Thankfully, the performances and the understated direction of Paul Lynch have aided in preventing this. It is a bit disconcerting, however, to see the rescue footage from the pilot (Vincent riding the top of the subway) being used so soon as stock footage, but it’s something that would be dropped from the show.

Important about this show, too, is that it helps to drive home the point that this format will allow for meaningful human drama to be intermixed with the Catherine-Vincent relationship.

Episode Four

Taped

"No Way Down"

Written by James Crocker

Directed by Thomas J. Wright

Catherine is walking down a dark alley, where she is surprised to see Vincent. He is there because he sensed her fear and wants to know why she's there. Her response is that she's meeting a witness, and the gamble is worth it. Alone, she goes into a a seedy building. A group of punks, led by a guy named Shake (Merritt Butrick) appear. He wants to know if talking to her will get his friend Willie "some slack." She says she'll do her best.

As the conversation continues, we learn that Shake was a witness to the beating death of a convenience store owner. Shake says that the guy they're talking about is named Chris, and that he's one of the chiefs of a gang called the Suits. Outside, members of the Suits arrive, and get out of their car, armed to the teeth with various weapons. One of them is concerned, stating that this "isn't our usual style." Chris believes that times have changed, and when someone pushes you, you have to push back...hard. They begin firing their weapons into the building, hitting Shake and his people. Vincent, who has been watching, growls and leaps out. He starts to help Shake, when a bomb is thrown into the building, effectively destroying it. Catherine lies unconscious in the street. The Suits, including Chris' retarded brother, proceed inside the building to see what's left.

Vincent awakens in the Suits' headquarters, to find himself chained up and the Suits taunting him, talking about his face and claws. The explosion has ruined Vincent's vision and hearing. He growls at them, but his being chained prevents their being too concerned.

The police arrive and question Catherine. She says there was no one else in there with her besides Shake and his people. Back with the Suits, Chris is demanding that Vincent howl for them. Vincent remains disoriented.

Catherine goes to the tunnels and speaks to one of the child-helpers, who tells her that Vincent went above and hasn't come back yet. Trying to control her panic, Catherine asks to be brought to Father. There, she tells him her fears that he might be hurt. Obviously pained, Father is near tears, wanting to know where this happened. Once told he wonders aloud what Vincent would be doing in the most dangerous place in the city for any of them. Catherine says that he was with her. Father bluntly says that her relationship with Vincent is a tragic mistake. Catherine wants his help, but there are only two tunnels that go to that part of the city. She asks him to show her where they are. Father pulls out some maps and begins to show her the locations of the tunnels, voicing his concern whether Vincent will be able to reach them.

This is the first direct scene between Father and Catherine, and it gives Roy Dotrice the opportunity to express all the anxiety he has felt towards the relationship between his "son" and this woman. It creates a nice bit of continuity that all along he has been advising Vincent against this romance, and now his warnings have bourne fruit.

Chris' retarded brother, Howie, approaches Vincent and asks him if he can talk, promising that he won't tell anyone. Vincent says he can and asks Howie to free him. Before anything can be done, the Suits come back into the room and chase him away from Vincent. Then they douse him in beer, and use a small torch to burn some fur. When one of the men smashes Vincent across the face with a crowbar and is about to strike again, Howie stops him. Howling, Vincent suddenly breaks free, throws some Suits away from him, smashes others into the walls and breaks out to freedom. But he is half blind, and his movements are slow.

This scene is very much like the one utilized in the original **King Kong**, where Kong is chained on stage in New York City for the press and the world to stare at in awe. While not exactly being tortured, he was nonetheless put through hell by man, and takes his first opportunity to break free and prove to all of them who's king of the city. What follows in "No Way Down" is as harrowing as Kong's making his way to the Empire State Building and scaling it before he is shot down.

Vincent makes his way into the street, his cloak hiding his facial features, and finds himself in the middle of traffic, with cars whizzing by him. Gradually he moves into an alley. Back inside, Chris has discovered that his big brother (not Howie) was killed by Vincent, and he's crying out for blood. Catherine, meanwhile, is searching the streets, and is met by Isaac, who immediately approaches a couple of winos and starts asking for information. He offers money to the man, who says the explosion woke him up and he saw the Suits drag someone out of the building and stuff him into the trunk of their car.

A cop comes down the alley with a flashlight, and finds Vincent, but does not see his features. The man is extremely friendly, as evidenced by his concern for Vincent's injuries. He pulls a flask out of his pocket and offers a "jolt" to Vincent, which he refuses. The man turns his back for a second, and when he turns around again, Vincent is gone.

The Suits continue searching the streets in their car, just as Catherine and Isaac search in a cab. Elsewhere, Vincent makes his way to a manhole cover and tries to open it. The Suits spot him in their rearview mirror and are trying to run him down. Howie does his best to grab the wheel, but the vehicle hits its intended target. Wounded, Vincent starts crawling away, his hand massaging what is probably broken ribs. He collapses, barely able to go on. Later, a woman is returning to her home, when she spots a collapsed Vincent and verbally threatens him, until she learns that he is hurt. She is about to call an ambulance, but he stops her from doing so. Again, his cloak covers his features. He begins to walk away, but collapses into her arms. She helps him into her apartment, and he sinks to the couch. The woman offers to look at his wounds, but he asks her not to. She turns out the light, catches sight of his face and backs away in fear. Without another word, he gets to his feet and leaves the apartment.

Once again, we are witness to a person whose life would appear to be somewhat miserable, and yet there is compassion within her. But, as is so often the case, she is frightened by that which she can't understand. Her concern is enveloped by fear. Thankfully she overcomes this as she pursues Vincent into the street and tells him that it's not safe for him to be outside. He'll be safer in her apartment, where she leads him. Vincent explains that he can't see, but he needs her help. Can she tell him how to get to an abandoned club nearby? She offers to take him there. Touched, Vincent asks her name and is told that it's Lucy. He thanks her, and the two of them are off.

Chris and the others are in a small park area, with Chris stating that he wants them to split up and look for the creature that killed his brother. Meanwhile, Catherine and Isaac discover the manhole cover Vincent had removed before the car had struck him. Catherine feels that he's still alive, which shocks Isaac. Judging by the skid marks, he'd say that they hit him at about fifty miles per hour.

Lucy is leading Vincent, when one of the female Suits spots him and starts screaming for Chris. Lucy sends Vincent off, serving as a distraction. One of the guys approaches her with a gun, wondering what she's doing out. Howie and the others join them. Chris wants to know where Vincent went. They force her to go with them as they search.

Vincent reaches the building he has been searching for and rips the entrance door off its hinges. One of the guys points a gun at him, but Vincent slams the steel door into the punk. They follow him into the building. Vincent tries to find his way to the entrance of the tunnel which will hold the key to sanctuary. Meanwhile, Chris tells them to split up. Vincent moves down a staircase and is shot at by one of the Suits. He stumbles and falls, trying to move to cover as soon as he reaches the bottom. Outside, the gunshots have been heard by Catherine and Isaac, who move into the building. Elsewhere, Lucy begins to weep. Isaac manages to overpower a couple of Suits, and they continue on their way. Vincent is pursued by one of the Suits into the tunnel area. He continues to shoot at him, then reloads his gun before continuing.

He continues his search in a corridor, where he is suddenly grabbed by Vincent. Needless to say, full retribution is dealt out to him! Vincent claws his face, slams his body against a wall like he was a rag doll, and then drops it lifelessly to the ground.

Howie suddenly walks behind Vincent and is nearly attacked, until he is recognized. Together Howie and Vincent open the door which leads into the underground cavern, identified mostly by the unending tapping sound of pipes. Chris is then behind them, his gun levelled. Chris is planning on shooting Vincent, but Howie doesn't want him to, and refuses to move. This doesn't stop Chris who cold bloodedly fires two shots into his brother. Before he dies, Howie embraces Chris and turns the gun on him before it's fired a third time. Both collapse lifelessly to the ground. Catherine and Isaac enter the room and catch sight of Vincent. She turns to Isaac and asks him to leave with "no questions." He does so, leaving them alone. Catherine and Vincent embrace and move slowly into the tunnel leading to the Underworld.

While being trapped in the above world is probably Vincent's greatest nightmare, "No Way Down" perhaps serves best as an example of the dual nature of our society, by focusing on both the good and the bad. We see examples of cold, callous human beings with no regard for life, and others who have been dealt a bad hand, but still manage to rise above their own personal pain to help others. We see it in Lucy, a prostitute willing to overcome her fear by lending a hand; the police officer who tried to help Vincent earlier; and even Howie who, though retarded, had more integrity and compassion in his heart than anybody else in the Suits. More than anything, this episode, despite all that Vincent endures, gives us hope.

By this point **Beauty and the Beast** was four for four, not a bad track record by any standard.

Episode Five

"Masques"

Written by George R.R. Martin

Directed by Alan Cooke

Trick or treaters come to Catherine's door. She gives them a treat and as they depart her father comes down the corridor, dressed in a Confederate soldier's uniform. It will be fifteen minutes, she tells him, before she's ready.

In the Underworld, Father is reading to a group of children. They sit enthralled, as does Vincent. Afterwards the children leave, with Vincent and Father discussing children's stories and their eternal appeal. The conversation turns more serious, as Father voices his concern over Vincent's decision to go to the surface.

"Surely on this night of all nights," Vincent replies in regards to Halloween, "I can walk among them."

Father is not convinced, although he has no choice in the matter. He merely asks Vincent to be careful. Vincent kisses him good-bye and begins his sojourn to the surface. Catherine, meanwhile, comes out of her room dressed as a Southern bell, and the two of them depart to a party in honor of Brigit O'Donnell.

An old man is about to close his costume shop, when a man almost forces the door open, demanding a costume. He gets a clown costume, changes into it, and while he's doing so we catch a glimpse of the gun in his pants. The store owner opens a newspaper and glances at a story announcing a Halloween party honoring Irish Peace Activist Brigit O'Donnell.

Later, at the party, Catherine and her father arrive and are introduced to Brigit O'Donnell. Outside, Vincent has scaled the wall and enters the party through the terrace. Inside again, Catherine's father is stopped by Brigit's bodyguard and his costume sword is taken away, with the explanation that there have been threats on the activist's life. Brigit, who has written a book entitled ***300 Days***, approaches them, explaining that the threats come from rebels who do not agree with the peace movement she has initiated in Ireland. Catherine catches sight of Vincent and excuses herself, but then can't find him.

Meanwhile, Vincent is mingling, fitting in perfectly, even to the point where a waiter asks if he'd like some caviar. Brigit approaches him, and the two strike up a conversation, with her noting that his costume is extraordinary. Vincent tells her that her writings have "helped him through dark times. They've touched me." He thanks her for the meaning her written words have brought him. Catherine then sees Vincent and Brigit stepping outside, and is a bit surprised. Once outdoors, Brigit describes the agony that war and acts of terrorism have brought to her people, and discusses her philosophy on life. She adds that her late husband and her tried to create a new world of peace, "but you know how it ended."

The man we saw earlier [described for now as the Clown] arrives at the party and cannot produce an invitation, so he will not be admitted. The Clown looks like he's going to start a fight, but he chooses, instead, to leave. Then he gets in line with a bunch of people and manages to get by the doorman. He immediately begins looking for Brigit. Elsewhere, Catherine is dancing with one Donald Pratt.

Outside the conversation is continuing between Brigit and Vincent. She says that she's being protected by bodyguards but wishes she could walk among the streets like a normal person, experiencing the world as everyone else does. Vincent, of course, can identify with this. When Brigit says she's cold, Vincent loans her his cloak. Brigit enters and goes to the elevator. The Clown enters another elevator and begins to pursue them. Vincent has gone to meet her outside so that they can walk the streets together, a special feeling of kinship having developed between them. The Clown continues his pursuit. Catherine and Pratt ask the doorman if he's seen the couple, and are told that they went into the park. They begin to follow.

Brigit senses Vincent's woman, and asks him about the woman that causes him pain. "She brings me such joy and such pain," he says, "as I have never known. I have no place in her world, she has no place in mine." She understands perfectly, being able to identify with her completely. She suggests that he forget he ever knew her to end the pain for both of them. He throws some of her own words back at her which contradict what she's just said. Brigit laughs, saying that such an act isn't fair. Then, Vincent senses the Clown's presence. He raises his gun and moves closer to where they were. Vincent steps out from beneath a tree and disarms him.

Catherine and Pratt find the unconscious form of the Clown. She sees Vincent, who, without a word, starts to walk away...alone. Brigit approaches Catherine and Pratt. The clown's name is Michael O'Fay, a "good IRA man." Brigit recognizes him as an enemy. Pratt then reveals himself to be an agent of Interpol, who was informed of an attempt on Brigit's life. Pratt goes off to get his car.

Going home, Vincent speaks with Father once again, wondering how mankind can hate so. Father has wondered about the same thing throughout his life.

Pratt is driving his car when O'Fay awakens. It turns out that her father is dying and wants to see her again, and O'Fay was sent to inform her of this. He wasn't after her, but was after the "fellow in the lion mask." At that exact moment, Catherine realizes that they're going the wrong way. Pratt pulls down a side street and into an underground garage. He stops and pulls a gun on the group. Vincent, still at home, senses this and departs. He is actually the man who was sent out to kill Brigit. He tells O'Fay to empty his pockets, which the man does. He tells him that his name is Jamie Harland, and that O'Fay is to pay for the death of his brother. The gun is fired, and O'Fay falls to the ground. He picks up a key for the hotel room of Brigit's father...a man he is determined to kill.

They go to the hotel, where Brigit is reunited with her father. Harland says that Michael O'Fay is burning in hell, where he will be soon. The man is not frightened, but cannot handle the announcement that Brigit will be killed first. Harland is about to pull the trigger when Catherine actually moves in for an attack, utilizing the training Isaac gave her. The gun flies into the air and lands on the bed. Brigit's father picks it up and is about to fire. Brigit tries to stop him, claiming that one death piled on top of another will solve nothing. If he's going to kill Harland, he's going to have to kill her too. The man cannot do it. Harland, being the slime of the earth that he is, suddenly grabs her, pulls a knife and starts to leave, using Brigit as a hostage. He takes several steps towards the door, and Vincent comes through the window, grabbing the man around the neck and throwing him viciously into the corridor. And like the Lone Ranger, he's gone.

The police arrive, and everyone goes outside. Catherine sees Vincent on the roof of the hotel. Turning her attention to Brigit, Catherine says she can arrange for her to spend some time with her father before he dies, despite the fact he's wanted by the police. "We must take what we can get," Brigit says optimistically. Catherine agrees, "Even if it's for one night."

Vincent then walks up to Catherine, checks out Brigit's wellbeing and is about to leave, but they realize that this is the one night they can walk freely among men. What follows is a beautiful montage of the city, as the couple experience St. Patrick's Cathedral, Rockefeller Center, Fifth Avenue, Times Square, the Statue of Liberty and so much more before dawn comes. They end up sitting before the Brooklyn Bridge, relating how beautiful the world really is. They begin to near each other for what will be their first kiss, when a jogger interrupts them, startled by Vincent's appearance. "Hey man," he laughs, "Halloween was yesterday."

The time has come for Vincent to return to the Underworld, and for Catherine to go home.

If "No Way Down" represents Vincent's ultimate nightmare, then "Masques" must be a dream come true for him, as it represents the one time a year when he can walk the streets without hiding himself.

Unfortunately the episode as a whole doesn't really hold together as well as its predecessors, despite the fact that Brigit's outlook on life closely mirrors that held by Vincent. Quite frankly, the storyline's politics just don't work in this format. The premise is an interesting one, but it simply seems out of place on this show. Proof of this can be found in the fact that the episode truly comes alive at the conclusion when Vincent and Catherine tour the city together. It really is a beautiful sequence of events, and one can only wish that this idea had been explored in more detail.

AN INTERVIEW WITH DIRECTOR ALAN COOKE

England's Alan Cooke has directed numerous television episodes in his native land, and has picked up the directorial reigns for numerous American shows, including ***Hart to Hart, Murder She Wrote, Beauty and the Beast*** *and* ***The Father Dowling Mysteries****. For* ***B & B*** *he has helmed the episodes "Terrible Savior" and "Masques," the former of which is significant in that it was the first episode to follow the pilot, and the latter because it represented the first time that Vincent could walk among men without fear. The following interview looks at these two particular shows from his point of view.*

Q:

When you first got involved, what did you think of the show's premise?

A:

I thought it was very fresh, very risky and very exciting.

Q:

Why risky?

A:

I think we were all quite concerned at the beginning as to whether it was going to take off or not. It was an intriguing idea, and I think the reason it worked is that it hit people on a mythic level. But on the surface, when people asked me what I was doing and I outlined it, they kind of raised an eyebrow. It didn't sound a very likely premise to take off. I thought it could work. I like anything to do with legend and fairy tale. I think they tap into the collective unconscious.

Q:

I think it's great that they've been able to so successfully intertwine our world with the Underground.

A:

I think a lot of that has to do with Ron Perlman, which was a wonderful stroke of casting.

Q:

What was your opinion of the script for "Terrible Savior?"

A:

I thought that was an interesting one. It gives a very good possibility of the mythic parallel because you had the two monsters, as it were. I thought it was a particularly successful link there.

Q:

The Vigilante, of course, has been a successful mainstay in our entertainment, whether that be on film or in literature.

A:

The Jason Walker character was most interesting to me, and formed a very nice reversal...mirror image...of the Beast. The Beast is fierce on the outside, and very gentle within, and Jason Walker was the other way around.

Q:

It was interesting that Jason got so swept up in the fantasy, that when he put on the mask, he believed he was the legend he was portraying.

A:

That's one of the remarkable things about the series. One doesn't expect popular television to explore the psyche to that extent, and I think that some of those overtones must have resonated for the audience, which is one of the reasons that it caught on as it did.

Q:

Watching the episode, one would think that it was particularly difficult to choreograph the fight scenes in such contained locales, such as the subway car and the bridge in the Underworld.

A:

The bridge was a big problem for us. We really didn't have room for anything that was described. The writer, George R.R. Martin, wrote with wonderful imagery and put it down on paper, describing how they would fight and fall from one bridge to the next, and one was to collapse and the abyss was below. But the studio was being reconstructed at that time, and what we had was the one area, and two principle sets which were Father's cave and Vincent's cave. We didn't actually shoot in Father's cave in that sequence. That was simply cannibalized. The bridge was put up some six feet off the ground, and then we had to devise ways to make it look like the area you saw in the episode. It created a series of very interesting problems. Of course we had that fantastic DP, Roy Wagner, on that, and he had some ideas, the set designer had some ideas, and we pooled our resources to make it work. We wanted it to be exciting, and yet the physical limitations of where we could shoot were considerable. I think the sound in that scene helped a lot. We did a lot of carefully thought out things with the sound which suggested the echoing and whispers from the other world, and so on.

Q:

Very suspenseful when Vincent nearly falls through the bridge and Jason is about to strike him down with his clawed hand.

A:

Then you come back to just the power of the actors' eyes. It was a moment of pure acting power, really.

Q:

Which has helped the show all along, actually.

A:

Right. And now that it's succeeded, it's quite nerve-wracking in a way to think of how completely it might *not* have succeeded if you had a less powerful man playing Vincent.

Q:

Do you think Linda Hamilton brings the same kind of intensity?

A:

I think she has considerable intensity as a player with a very interesting color and quality.

Q:

Your only other episode was "Masques." What did you think of the story for that one?

A:

That was one they were most anxious about. They asked me to do it because they felt I had an intuitive sense of what the Beast was. That was one of the trickiest ones because it involved his appearing in public, almost unmasked, as it was. The nice concept is that on Halloween night he can walk around and everyone would think it was a cute make-up. At the same time, the producers were very concerned, because in a sense it tested the theory to the outermost. They were always afraid that it would look like a man wearing a cat mask. So suddenly here he was being able to walk around because he looked like a man wearing a cat mask. It sort of ripped the seams of the entire concept, and reminded us that it was just an actor, and they always wanted to keep around Vincent this aura of mystery that he was not a man who was dressed up; that he was not really a human at all. That was a nice challenge.

Q:

Perlman makes you believe that Vincent actually exists.

A:

Absolutely. He plays the role with such authority.

Q:

Did you think the politics of the episode worked?

A:

Oh yes, I think so. They were only kind of slightly sketched. Again, it was unusual to me that they really did go into more than just the surface of some of these important problems of today.

Q:

Of the two episodes, which do you personally prefer?

A:

I like "Terrible Savior" very much. It was so close to the beginning and a great deal of care was put into it by all departments. I don't mean to suggest that care wasn't put into the second one, but it was the first time for us all in many ways. I really like that. I like everything about it, as well as the contrast between the violence and the lovely scenes between the Beast and Catherine.

Episode Six

"The Beast Within"

Written by Andrew Laskos

Directed by Paul Lynch

We begin on a loading dock, where a man in a sports car drives up to the foreman. The man asks about Flynn and is told that "he's still making noises." He says ominously that enough is enough and departs. The foreman tells Flynn to go to a certain area, which he does. Another man follows as they prepare for a multi-ton crate that is being moved. Suddenly Flynn is knocked to the ground, the crate is dropped and the man is crushed to death. There is a witness to the crime, who, frightened, moves away from the area.

Vincent is in a decaying hotel, standing over an old, feverish man, who obviously knows him. Sam, it turns out, is a helper to the Underground who is dying, but he advises Vincent not to return because "Mitch is back." This news obviously disturbs Vincent. Nonetheless, Vincent points out that Sam has always been there for the Underground, and they will be there for him.

In the DA office Catherine is reading case files regarding the dock we'd seen earlier. Union officials are there. Joe Maxwell approaches her, explaining that the mob is making "big moves" against the union. After telling her that the case is a dangerous one, but acknowledging that she can handle it, Joe tells Catherine that she's on it. She goes into the DA office where she meets Franke DeCorsia, the head of the local union. He explains that the mob is trying to turn the clock back again, a job they think will be made easier by Mitch Denton, an enforcer on the docks several years earlier. He adds that Charlie Flynn was willing to testify, but "Denton got to him first."

DeCorsia brings Catherine down to the dock to meet some of the people who were there when Flynn was murdered. Naturally they don't want to talk to her, and none of them have seen anything. As the couple walk out of the office, DeCorsia witnesses one of the mob enforcers harassing some of his men. He runs over, knees him, and tells the man to get the hell off of the dock, and to pass the message on to his boss.

That evening, Vincent and Catherine stand outside on her terrace, and he can feel the turmoil within her. She says that she has the chance to make a difference; to help honest men keep their jobs. Admittedly Catherine is afraid, but Vincent assures her she has the strength and the courage to handle this job. He only wishes that he could always be there with her. "You are," she smiles.

Two punks break into Sam's room, demanding to know where the money is. They move in to stab him, when Mitch Denton runs in and quickly disposes of the two of them, then runs over to Sam, who he refers to as "Pop." Apparently he heard that his father was sick, so he came by to see him. While in prison, Mitch admits, he had a lot of time to think, and he simply doesn't want Sam to hate him. He wants to move him out of this place so that he can take care of him, but Sam says he's already got people to take care of him. "Who?" Mitch sneers. "Vincent?" In the ensuing conversation, we learn that Mitch spent five years in jail because "Vincent wouldn't let me hide out in those tunnels until the heat blew over." It's obvious that the man has not forgiven Vincent for his "crime," and the impression is that revenge will be extracted. Going outside, Mitch locates an entrance to the Underworld and climbs through. As he walks down a corridor, one of the Helpers catches sight of him.

Vincent and Father are discussing a fresh underground spring that has just been discovered, when a Helper runs towards them, explaining that Luke saw an intruder in the tunnels. Vincent is off in a flash, eventually catching up to Mitch, who says that he decided to "visit."

"You're not welcome here," says Vincent sternly, while at the same time acknowledging the friendship they had—when they were children. Mitch had lived in the tunnels for eight years as a boy, until he "betrayed" their trust and looked for the easy life above ground. He made his way on to the docks where he made a living by serving as an enforcer for the mob. He finally leaves.

Vincent and Father start working on changing the tunnel entrances. Father is pained by Mitch's return, feeling guilty that perhaps he should have spent more time with him, counseled him more...but Vincent says that he, too, feels that way. Yet when he tried to find the face of the boy he knew, all he saw instead was hatred.

Catherine is in a bar with DeCorsia. Jack Sweeney, the man who actually witnessed Flynn's death, shows up, angry that Catherine is there. Finally he says, "I have to think about my family...I'm sorry." Catherine says they could arrange witness protection, but Sweeney says that he's already said too much. DeCorsia and Catherine leave, each going to their own cars. Suddenly his explodes, instantly killing the man within.

Devastated, Catherine is at home when she hears a tapping on the terrace door. Vincent is there because he felt that death almost took her, and he says she should go no further with her investigation. She says she can't just drop it, especially now. She feels that she has no choice but to bring the men responsible down. Vincent softly says that he doesn't know if he could handle anything happening to her as the loneliness of life alone would be unbearable.

Catherine arrives at Sweeney's home, which is a bit surprising to him. The man's wife invites her in to sit down, and tells him to listen to Catherine, noting that "this time we're in this together." Catherine argues more strongly, and Sweeney's kids even get involved in the conversation, telling him to stand up to Mitch Denton. He tries to explain what his testifying would mean in terms of moving away, but the kids throw his previous advice right back at him: doing what's right is hard sometimes. Sweeney nods and says that he will testify.

Catherine gets into her car and drives off. Denton is in another car, having staked out the man's house. Next day, Sweeney goes to the DA office and tells them everything he knows. Elsewhere, Denton is meeting with a couple of men from the dock, saying that they have to do something to Sweeney that will send out a message to everyone else. At Sweeney's house, Catherine is helping the family pack up their belongings. Outside, Denton's car pulls up and he and the men are about to get out. When several squad cars pull up to the house, they pull away very casually.

Catherine goes home and as she approaches her door, Mitch Denton and his men step out of a doorway. They take her out of the building and into their car. Denton demands to know where Sweeney is. Vincent, in the tunnels, has detected this, and is once again on his way to help. Catherine karate chops Mitch across the throat and runs out of the car. She pulls out a gun and fires back at one of Mitch's men. Denton himself fires a shot that drops Catherine. Vincent arrives and, panicking, Denton runs back to his car. Cradling her body in his arms, Vincent lets out a horrific howl before bringing her body to the hospital, leaving it outside so no one can see him. "Don't die, Catherine," he whispers. "If you die, so do I." He departs shortly before someone finds her body. Cutting through the tunnels, Vincent begins running as he's never run before.

Mitch is with his men on the docks, frightened that Vincent will come after him. His men are armed, ready to fire at anything that moves. Taking a cue from Rambo, Vincent starts taking care of the men, one by one. He grabs the first and effortlessly breaks his neck. He smashes the second across the face. The third is attacked off camera, his slashed body slowly making its way up the stairs. Mitch backs away until he stops against a wall. Suddenly Vincent's arm smashes through the wall next to him and knocks him down. He comes through completely, howling madly, sounding more like an enraged lion than we've ever heard before. Vincent starts closing the gap with Mitch. They're on a catwalk, and Mitch starts to weep and beg him not to hurt him. We intercut with the hospital. Catherine awakens and calls his name out weakly. Vincent "hears" this, and stops his howling. The hatred immediately flows out of his body and he looks compassionately down upon Mitch Denton. "There's nothing left of you," he says softly. "Nothing." The impression we're left with is that Mitch has lost his mind, as he sits shivering on the catwalk.

Catherine reawakens in the hospital room to see Vincent, who has climbed in through the window. She says she was having a dream that the two of them were walking down Fifth Avenue, the sky was blue and he bought her ice cream. She falls to sleep again, with Vincent standing lovingly over her.

"The Beast Within" is an effective enough episode, marred only by the fact that it seems to be lacking the romantic passion of some of the earlier episodes. One would imagine that the maintaining of that element week after week would be extremely difficult, if not impossible, to do. It would have been nice to be given perhaps a little bit more on the relationship between Vincent and Mitch aside from the one scene. Once again we were provided a little more insight into the Underworld in terms of its purpose. As Vincent said, Mitch was given the chance for a better life beneath the surface, but the man could not handle the idea of "living like a rat."

As we would soon discover, this "tunnel life" is actually something of a utopia.

Episode Seven

Taped

"Nor Iron Bars a Cage"

Written by Howard Gordon and Alex Ganza

Directed by Thomas J. Wright

A couple is jogging through Central Park, the focus of someone's video camera. The man (Professor Edward Hughes) holding the camera is trying to get shots of owls, but locks on to the image of Vincent for a moment. Then the figure is gone. Going back to his lab, he reviews the tape, and sees a fairly clear image of Vincent's face beneath the cloak. This is obviously a stunning experience for him.

Next day, Catherine is discussing a wife abuse case with Joe Maxwell. Saying that a warrant will be sent out for the woman's husband. Changing the subject, he hands a letter to Catherine which says that the DA from Rhode Island wants her to move there and work for him. "We're not just talking about a promotion here," says Joe, "we're talking a quantum leap in your career." This is surprising to Catherine, who doesn't know what to do. Does she want to change her life so drastically? Whatever her decision, it has to be made by the next day.

Edward Hughes is discussing his discovery with his superiors, but they don't see anything in the professor's photographs and videotapes. In the conversation we recognize the conflict that exists between he and them, as they discuss the fact that fifteen years earlier someone received the recognition for work that he had performed, and it has haunted him since. They, unfortunately, believe that he's merely feeling sorry for himself, and refuse to acknowledge this latest discovery as anything but what it appears to be: nothing. Edward's peers leave the room, while an unidentified man stares into it through a window outside.

Catherine goes to the Underground to see Vincent and tells him of the decision that she needs to make. Although it pains him, Vincent tries to be philosophical, telling her that she must go and experience "everything you were meant to do, for me...for both of us...and then, I can truly be with you...always." She wants to know if there's any other way, but his response is that there isn't—for them.

This scene, as short as it is, is fantastic, and while we can feel the pain being experienced by both Catherine and Vincent, we also get a feeling of hope that *someday* these lovers will be together in every way. It would seem that Vincent is essentially telling her to experience all that she can in the world; accomplish all that she wants to, and only then will she be able to accept, or reject, the love they feel for each other. As he plaintively notes, his world is the Underground and the confines of the city. There is no existence for him outside of it. Not in our society.

Going off alone after Catherine leaves, Vincent collapses against a wall, chest heaving mightily, emotionally distraught. Catherine, meanwhile, goes to see Joe Maxwell and tells him that she's going to go to Providence. Joe is a little disappointed, having hoped that she might have refused, but they hug each other in congratulations.

Father and Vincent are in a heated debate over the situation, with Vincent stating that Catherine has changed his life forever, and without her he will be lost. Father counters, stating that he should accept the changes, but allow the woman to pursue her own destiny. Naturally, as based on his previous conversation with Catherine, Vincent is aware of this, but convincing his heart is quite another story.

Professor Hughes is reading over some papers, when the man we had seen earlier steps into his office, identifies himself as a grad student named Jonathan Gould, one of his pupils, explains that he was outside his office and believes in what Hughes says he discovered. Gould says he wants to discover the truth of the creature. Hughes, who has tried to convince himself that what he saw doesn't exist, suggests they forget it. Gould continues pressing, saying that he has the resources to help prove that this creature does indeed exist.

Vincent comes out of the tunnel area and begins walking through the park, when he is shot with two tranquilizer darts. He makes a valiant attempt at escape, but the drugs take effect, and he collapses to the ground, unconscious. High above, an old woman staring into the park via telescope, has seen the whole thing.

Catherine is packing up her belongings, and finds her copy of **The Sonnets of William Shakespeare**, a nice bit of continuity from an earlier episode. There is a knock upon the door, and when she opens it there is a note from the Underground which explains that Father needs to speak to her. Soon thereafter she is making her way through the tunnels, and meets with him. He explains that Vincent has been missing for two days, and they have no idea where he might be. Father adds that "Vincent was not himself after he spoke to you." She says that both Vincent and she felt strongly about her leaving being the best thing. Nodding, Father responds that they must find him, wherever he may be. Catherine pauses for a moment, wanting to know why he contacted her. "Because I know you care," he responds softly.

Another great moment, and a real turning point in the relationship between Father and Catherine. He has gone from continually protesting the relationship that exists between his son and her, to the point where he is accepting it. The next step, which would come later, would be the endorsing of it. What's so effective about a scene like this is that it showcases a continual growth in the characters.

Hughes and Gould are studying the monitors they have hooked up to Vincent, who lies on a lab table. They are amazed by all they have witnessed, with Huges noting that he is human. Gould doesn't agree, pointing out the different features between Vincent and humans, and classifying him, without hesitation, as an animal. Their differences continue as Hughes wants to gather all the information they can, while Gould wants to make a public statement the next day. Hughes won't go for it, believing that history will repeat itself; that, in effect, the government would take Vincent away, leaving him with nothing...again. Gould, whose face clouds over, says that the beast is theirs, and the two of them will decide what is to be done.

Catherine is home, again, staring upon the city, hoping that Vincent is okay. Back at the lab, Vincent is having a dream which registers on the lab equipment. In the dream, he is in Catherine's apartment, searching for her. Then she is there, smiling in front of him. He goes towards her and she vanishes, leaving Vincent all alone. Saying her name, he comes awake, finding himself strapped to the table, a light shining above.

Hughes has heard his voice and goes to Gould, who doesn't accept the signs of intelligence and is intent on keeping him tranquilized. At that moment, Vincent breaks free and starts to get up. Gould grabs a tranquilizer pistol and fires two darts into Vincent's chest, sending him, once again, down.

Edie visits Catherine, who tells her that she's beginning to have a change of heart, but isn't sure. Edie picks up the Shakespeare book and reads the inscription by Vincent, but Catherine doesn't want to talk about this person, aside from noting that he is part of the reason for her having second thoughts. Then Catherine takes note of a sleazoid paper (ala ***The National Enquirer***) which Edie brought her, particularly the headline which reads "Grandma Sees

Monster Captured." She picks it up and starts reading the story.

Vincent is awake and in a large cage. Time passes through a series of dissolves, with Vincent growing more and more depressed. Once again it should be noted how effective Ron Perlman is in this role: he conveys the image of a depressed dog or cat, who just lies there with no interest in anything, his chest heaving quickly. The primary difference is that a thin tear has rolled down his cheek. Going on at the same time is yet another debate between Hughes and Gould, who notes that a) he was indeed after the truth, but, b) the truth is not something which should be horded like a secret. He turns to Hughes and hopes that the man's belief that this creature has a soul is wrong, particularly for Vincent's sake. "I hope he's an imbecile," Gould says, "because, like it or not, the world is about to make a circus act out of him." Hughes tries to stop him from leaving, but Gould effortlessly throws him aside and leaves. Vincent notes all of this quietly.

Later, Gould returns with one of Hughes' superiors and is stunned to find that Vincent is gone. Meanwhile, Catherine Chandler goes into the sleazoid's main office, and questions the writer of the story, demanding to know where the woman lives. We switch to that woman's apartment, where Catherine is now talking to her. This woman, we learn, is something of a voyeur, always staring down upon the park and making note of the many strange things she has seen. Catherine asks her about the night she saw the "monster" being captured. With the information she has obtained from the woman, Catherine goes down to the tunnel area where Vincent was captured, and finds the pair of darts he had ripped out of his chest before collapsing.

Hughes, who has moved to another area, is talking to the still-caged Vincent, begging that he let him help. The best help he can be is to release him. Hughes rejoices that this beast can speak, but wants to know why he refused to speak in front of Gould."The other man means me harm," he replies simply, "and no words would change that." They introduce themselves to each other. They talk a moment about Catherine, and when asked what he is, Vincent replies that he is merely what he is, and that if pricked he will bleed, if struck he will strike back, and if caged he will die. This obviously touches Hughes, but he is confused as to what he should do. Vincent once again pleads that he be freed, but Hughes is unable to do so at this time. Vincent announces that he's dying.

Catherine goes to Hughes' office the next day and shows him the darts she retrieved. Their serial numbers were traced from the supplier to Hughes, and she wants to know where Vincent is. He can't take her to him, his entire reputation..maybe the rest of his life...is at stake. This is astounding to Catherine. Can Vincent's pain be worth all that? Her tone turns more pleading, explaining that she and Vincent are connected in some way that even she doesn't understand, and that he represents the best of what it means to be human, but if his freedom is taken away, then the thing that makes him most human will be gone as well. This does the trick, as she's brought to him. Hughes is about to open the cage door, when Gould steps out of the darkness, demanding the key to the cage.

A fist fight develops between Gould and Hughes, who is ultimately stabbed by the other man. The key is thrown into Catherine's hands. Gould moves towards her, Vincent stands up in the cage. Gould wraps his arms around her and literally tries to shake the key from her grasp. Catherine pushes off of one wall, which sends the two of them backwards and against the cage. Vincent reaches out and breaks Gould's neck (off-camera, mind you). Catherine opens the cage, but Vincent's first concern is Hughes. Catherine runs over to him, but the man, who's dying, tells her to take Vincent away, wishing that he had had the opportunity to get to know him better. He begs Vincent's forgiveness as life leaves his body.

In the Underground, Catherine is reading to Vincent a passage which succinctly states that she has no intention to leave the city...or him.

Despite a couple of story contrivances (the old woman who just *happens* to be a voyeur, and the darts which Hughes and Gould have so conveniently left behind for Catherine to discover) and the repetition of "No Way Down's" theme of Vincent being trapped on the surface, "Nor Iron Bars A Cage" is terrific. The cast is in fine form; writers Gordon and Ganza have given us a touching story; the direction of Thomas J. Wright successfully conveys the pathos of the script.

There is an interesting parallel in some instances to Steven Spielberg's **E.T.** in that Vincent represents the same dream come true for Hughes as E.T. did for the NASA scientist who befriends young Elliot. It's a sense of having the subject of our dreams in hand, but choosing to let it go so that it can live its own life and keep its freedom. Another analogy that can be found is Vincent's dying because of his captivity, much as the extraterrestrial did in that film.

Thankfully the series was still trying different directions, allowing the cast of characters to continue growing, which, in turn, keeps it that much more interesting for the audience. One last thing to note: by this point, one can feel one's self wanting the two of them to kiss already. Alas, the frustration would continue throughout the rest of the season.

Episode Eight

Taped

"Song of Orpheus"

Written by Howard Gordon and Alex Ganza

Directed by Peter Medak

A barber shop proprietor's last customer leaves the premises, and the man sits down to read the paper. In the classified section his attention is caught by an ad which begins, "The Wreck of My Memories." He clips this out, places it in a bottle and deposits that bottle into a drain pipe some blocks away.

In the Underground, Vincent and Father are enjoying a game of chess. Dustin, one of the children of this realm, delivers the bottled note. Father extracts it and reads the message. His reaction is immediate and emotional. Vincent detects this and questions him. After a moment's hesitation, Father explains that the things he told him about the world above were all true, but he has kept secret certain aspects of his life before he moved to the Underground. Now he has to return as soon as he can, and plans to return that evening. "When I return," he says, "we'll talk." Vincent tries to obtain further information, but Father will not talk further.

A woman named Margaret rests in a hospital bed, her lawyer Alan Taft explaining that her "pointless" message has run for seven days, and he wants to take it out of the paper. She refuses, pointing out that a day hasn't passed that her thoughts did not move to the target of the ad. This angers her companion, who says that "he" (Father) dropped off the face of the Earth some thirty five years earlier. She is convinced that the man is still alive. There is a knock on the door, and a man named Henry walks in, bearing flowers. It's obvious that he and the lawyer don't get along.

Father dresses in a suit he hasn't worn in thirty five years and makes his way to the surface, this obviously being a dramatic decision he's making. Back on the surface, Henry meets with Alan, the lawyer, to discuss Margaret. In their conversation we learn that six months earlier Margaret was diagnosed as having pancreatic cancer, and Henry, the head of a charitable organization, began soliciting her for a huge donation, so that she will be remembered. Alan is worried about Henry. Some checking has been done, and he has learned that Henry is not the financially trustworthy person he pretends to be. Alan'll keep his discovery quiet, provided that Henry pull back from Margaret immediately, severing all ties. "You're an old man, Alan," sneers Henry. "You don't want to lock horns with me." Henry leaves the office.

Father climbs out of a subway entrance and is immediately assaulted by culture-shock, including break dancers, modern fashions, the Hard Rock Cafe and the city in general. He has a brief flashback to his being hauled out of the Justice Building, but no further explanation is given.

Eventually he makes it to Alan's office. The door is ajar, and when he enters the room he unknowingly triggers a silent electronic alarm. Moving further into the office he is horrified to find Alan's dead body, papers scattered all around him. At that exact moment, the police run in, weapons levelled at him.

Vincent arrives at Catherine's apartment and taps gently on the terrace door. She awakens, steps outside and is told that Father is missing. Vincent needs her help, which she's only too happy to provide. Catherine asks about Father's former life. All Vincent knows is that he was a doctor; not even his real name. Meanwhile, Father is being processed at the police station.

Vincent returns to the Underground, not sure of what he should be doing. We can see that Father's disappearance is tearing him apart. He begins to go through Father's desk drawers, closets and cabinets, looking for *anything* that might provide some answers. Vincent discovers a name tab of the institute Father used to work at, as well as a wedding photo of Father and Margaret.

At the police station, the cops haven't found any identification, but what items they have found in the man's pockets include a silver certificate which hasn't been made in over thirty years and ticket stubs for a *Brooklyn* Dodgers game. They begin interrogating him, asking why he killed Alan Taft. Father says he didn't, and they want to know what he was doing there. Father doesn't respond and their patience is wearing thin. They've found the classified ad and they want to know what it means. What's his name? The questions don't stop.

Father looks at one of the cops and flashes back to the Fifties when he was being asked if he had ever been a member of the Communist party. In the flashback we learn that he was a research physicist who tried to inform people that the Atomic Energy Commission had miscalculated the effects of radiation on human beings. Because of this, he was classified by his superiors as a Communist, and blacklisted.

Back in the present, he still hasn't said a word to the police in response to their questions.

Catherine is doing research at the library in her building with Vincent, looking back at the newspaper files concerning Father, whose real name was Doctor Jacob Welles. As seen in the flashback, Welles (Father) did his best to halt research on atomic weapons because of their harm to humans. They also learn that Welles was blacklisted. Vincent holds in his hands an envelope with Magaret's name and address on it. He hasn't opened it, but hands it over to Catherine, who does open it and reads aloud from it. Margaret was sent to Paris by her father who wouldn't let her stay with a Communist. The man had their marriage annulled. Margaret had written that she didn't fight her father's decision, because although she knew Welles was innocent, she didn't have the strength to stand by him. She also pleaded that Welles not hate her for it, and states that she clings to "the wreck of my memories."

Next day, Catherine is at Margaret's house, talking to Henry. Unfortunately Margaret is supposedly too ill to see her, and Henry suggests that Catherine come back the next day. He offers to help her with whatever she needs help with, but Catherine says that it's private. Henry doesn't like the sound of that. When Catherine leaves, he sends Connors, one of the men working in the house, after her to find out exactly what she wants. Henry goes in to see Margaret, who acts extremely drugged. Henry is intent on keeping her that way.

Back at work, Catherine is in the midst of talking to Joe Maxwell, who points out that she's fifteen minutes late for a deposition. Enroute through the prison block Catherine is shocked to find Father in one of the cells. Seeing her, the man turns away, embarrassed. Catherine continues to the cell of her appointed prisoner, to take his statement. Later, Catherine pays a visit to Father, and they begin talking. Father asks her to please stay out of the situation. Catherine points out that he's been charged with murder, and she's the only one who can help him. Catherine confesses her knowledge of his past life, and notes that Vincent is aware of it as well. Father explains that he didn't wish to keep things from his "son," but merely wanted to forget. She says that she tried to see Margaret, but couldn't get in because Margaret was too ill. They discuss the message in the newspaper, which supposedly translates to Margaret wanting to see him again. Alan, he adds, defended him during the "witch hunts, and put his own reputation on the line."

Vincent is on the bridge we'd seen in "Terrible Savior," contemplating the situation. He begins moving through the tunnels again, and hears clanging on pipes which apparently translates to an urgent message. Vincent meets with a child Helper, who hands him the message that Father is okay.

Back at work, Catherine and Edie are discussing Henry Dutton, who seems to be a truly charitable individual, having been involved in everything from the Peace Corps to homes for the homeless. That night, Catherine goes to Alan Taft's building, and is watched by Henry and Connors. Entering the man's office, Catherine starts to look around for clues she can use to learn the truth behind Alan's death. Catherine starts going his files and finds information pertaining to Henry Dutton, including the material which Alan threatened Dutton with earlier. As Catherine leaves the building, she is grabbed by Dutton and Connors.

Catherine is being held at Margaret's house, where she confronts Dutton with her discovery that the man has been funnelling millions of dollars donated to charity into his own private account. Dutton feels no guilt at all, and cryptically says that he plans on killing her as well. The amount of money they're talking about makes it all worthwhile to him.

They take her into an elevator and start the ride back down to the street. Vincent, we learn, is on top of it, and pulls just the right cable to make the device stop where it is. Catherine knocks the two men away from her, just as Vincent rips off the top of the elevator and pulls her out of it and into the shaft. She wraps herself on his back, and Vincent, carrying Catherine, begins climbing up the cable to safety.

We dissolve to Catherine and Father entering the subway entrance, having proved the man's innocence. Before he departs, Father says, "Catherine, you've been more than a good friend to us. I know what you've risked, and believe me, I am grateful." As the man starts down the stairs, Catherine calls out, telling Father that she would never hurt Vincent because she loves him. Father says he's aware of this. It can only bring Vincent unhappiness "Because part of him is a man," Father says softly, continuing down the stairs.

Father returns to the Underworld where Vincent embraces him, and then Father is reunited with Margaret, who Vincent has brought down. Father and Margaret hug each other passionately, desperately trying to make up for thirty five years in the brief time that remains before illness takes her life away. Margaret believes that the cancer is God's way of paying her back for what she did to him.

Father says that he's forgiven everything, although there had been a time when he gorged himself on bitterness and self-pity. Then he "came to know someone who had every reason to curse fate... to feel punished, and yet he accepted all that life had to offer with gratitude and love." Naturally he's speaking of Vincent.

Later, Vincent is meeting with Catherine, telling her that Margaret's final week was the happiest of her life, and Father is now healing himself from the pain. Catherine feels that it is extremely sad that their lives together had a beginning and an end, but no middle. Vincent points out that they had seven days....

Suffice to say, there isn't a dry tear in the living room when this episode concludes, and for good reason. "Song of Orpheus" is a tale that successfully conveys the joy of obtaining love, the pain of losing it and the agonizing frustration of never being able to *truly* share it.

As stated earlier in this volume, one of the most important ingredients making up the success of **Beauty and the Beast** is its extremely strong supporting cast. It is to the credit of the producers, as well as Hamilton and Perlman, that the scenarists can write scripts which cater to characters other than the leads. Such stories tend to make these people much more clearly defined and, in the long run, help to sustain the reality of the story. Roy Dotrice excels as Father in this episode. We can see the relationship between his character and Catherine beginning to deepen, despite the way he looks down at her relationship with Vincent. At least now we're hearing his reason for doing so: part of Vincent is a man.

Episodes like "Song of Orpheus" help to prove why **Beauty and the Beast** has succeeded, where so many shows have failed.

Two views of Ron Perlman: in and out of makeup.
Actor Ron Perlman brings the Beast to life.
Photos courtesy Witt/Thomas Productions
in cooperation with Republic Pictures.

The fabulous Linda Williams, and the Beast is always near.
Photos courtesy Witt/Thomas Productions in cooperation with Republic Pictures.

Roy Dotrice portrays Father, Vincent's surrogate parent, and founder of the Underground.
Photos courtesy Witt/Thomas Productions in cooperation with Republic Pictures.

ABOVE: Ren Woods portrays Edie, Catherine's friend, and a computer operator in the DA's office.
BELOW: The Deputy District Attorney, Catherine's boss, as played by Jay Acovone.

AN INTERVIEW WITH HOWARD GORDON

*During the first season of **Beauty and the Beast**, Howard Gordon, teamed with partner Alex Gansa, became story editor of the series, and penned some of the finest episodes. For the second season, both have been promoted to the position of Associate Producer.*

*The following interview with Gordon took place in the middle of **Beauty and the Beast's** first year.*

Q:

What has the atmosphere on the show been like?

A:

We're all very excited. It's nice, for one thing, to get the numbers, which bears out the fact that we've got a "commercial" audience. But the critical acclaim makes it doubly exciting. So I think the atmosphere here is very excited. It's one of the most diverse and comfortable staffs I think I've ever seen. Ron Koslow is a feature writer, George Martin is a novelist...it's a very interesting and positive creative atmosphere.

Q:

Have you been involved since the beginning?

A:

Alex and I weren't involved with the pilot, but we came on right after that, in June. We screened the pilot and were invited on aboard.

Q:

When you hear the idea of the show, it sounds almost too bizarre to work.

A:

Absolutely. We felt that way in the beginning, although I knew Koslow from his work in the movies and that he was a top screenwriter. I also knew that Witt-Thomas is a very prestigious, small company, sort of like a mini-MTM. So I knew there had to be something more to it, and having screened the pilot we realized we were right. And the acting...Perlman was just really fantastic, and we wanted to write for him.

Q:

So what's the appeal for you?

A:

It's different. We've only been writing for two years, but we've sort of had our fill of cops and robbers and car crashes. This really had a kind of romance and it harkened back to a sort of former age. It just appealed to us on a real visceral level, the fact that there was this really deep romance and he was this creature who was a hero for our time. A new hero, basically. That's what appealed to us. It was different from anything we had ever seen, and it was a New York show, too, which was appealing.

Q:

Well, only the pilot was actually shot in New York.

A:

Believe it or not, one of the things that sort of got us hooked was that at the time we came on, there was the possibility we were going to move back to New York, and that to me was real important. They even talked to Mayor Koch about lowering the production cost. The unions are very tight over there and very prohibitive, and they were negotiating with Koch because they really wanted the show to be there, but none of the unions would bend. So for the budget we were given, it would have been impossible to do. It's ironic, because the whole story is really about the magic of the city. I think in an ideal world, if we were shooting in New York, we would be able to relate the differences between the city and the underworld better. If New York is a microcosm of the world, then this sort of semi-Utopia below the city of New York speaks of the fact that there is a civilization somewhere in New York, which is the craziest of places.

Q:

I think that's summed up, too, with the opening shot of the pilot where we see a tree, hear birds chirping, see the words "Once Upon A Time..," we pull back and we're in Manhattan.

A:

Absolutely. It's interesting because the tone of the show is two-tier. We really wanted to portray the above world as realistically as possible. Even if almost stylized, we wanted to emphasize the grittiness, speed and fast pace, in counterpoint to the real lyrical, soft-toned underworld. So in a broad thematic level, that's what we're trying to do. We're making every effort to keep this show unique. We don't want it to be **Starsky and the Beast**. When people saw the pilot the general reaction was, "I hope Vincent isn't crashing through walls every week."

Q:

I think that's a legitimate concern.

A:

It's very legitimate, and it certainly was ours. We made it very clear when we came on the show that we didn't want to write **The Incredible Hulk**. The key word then, as it is now, is romance. Every week should always try to push forth the story of Vincent and Catherine, and how these people, who are involved in an impossible, unconsummatable—is that a word?—love, and what they do.

Q:

But will that turn into schtick after a while?

A:

Even freelancers having seen the pilot have said, "Gee, I love the pilot, but where the hell is the show going to go?" Even after having gone twelve episodes into the season, we're still kind of asking ourselves that question. It's an exploration; a learning experience for us that are even on staff, because we're just not entirely sure where the relationship can go. We do have every intention of getting a little bit wilder in the second half (of the first season). We're going to explore the Underworld a little bit more, and what goes on there. It was because of the network's fear that we stayed away from the Underworld for the first twelve shows, because science fiction and fantasy have been bad words on network television. The genre hasn't worked, so, traditionally, it's been a bad word.

Q:

What will we see?

A:

We're learning that the Underworld is a place for different people, and for different people it means different things. For some people, it's a place of healing, it's a way station for when the world above is really too much to handle for whatever reason. For instance, an episode which Alex and I just wrote involves a deaf girl who was abandoned as a child by her parents. She's been raised in the world below, and she ends up witnessing a murder on one of her runs above. The question is, does she testify or remain below? The whole point is that this is a girl who's becoming a young woman, so her coming up to testify is a metaphor for her whole process of emerging as a woman. It is, in fact, time for her to leave the Underworld, so we're going to trace this woman's particular story. Hopefully if we find enough stories, the Underworld, again...it's function, rather, would be more defined. Why would people want to live beneath the Earth? We're asking ourselves that question and coming up with some wonderfully interesting answers. We're going to get a little wild, and do a different type of show.

Q:

But always with the romantic core to it?

A:

Right. When we came on, Ron Koslow said that, as a model, he thought of **Naked City**, and he wanted our main characters to sort of be vehicles in relating to the guest stars' shows, and hopefully each story which happens each week will harken back to, or resonate with, the Vincent-Cathy relationship. I'm particularly proud of the ones that Alex and I did.

Q:

You've done three in a row, right?

A:

Yeah, and the one I'm most proud of is "An Impossible Silence," with the deaf girl.

Q:

Ron Perlman has gone on record as saying that he loves that episode, as well as the role.

A:

He's great. His excitement about the show is just contagious.

Q:

How did you enter the writing field?

A:

Alex and I graduated from Princeton in 1984, and we were both in the creative writing department...program...in the English Department. We had both won a fellowship for fiction writing, and decided one night to move to Los Angeles. That summer we wrote a **St. Elsewhere** spec script. In December of '84, we'd gotten the script to John Wilder, who was the executive producer of what was going to become **Spenser for Hire**. It was just a pilot at that point. He liked our script and six months later we wrote our first episode. We wrote a total of six, and then did some work on **Houston Knights** and **The Wizard**. Eventually, through John Wilder, our scripts got to Tony Thomas, who passed them on to Ron Koslow, who hired us. And that's the nutshell version of it. I have dozens of friends around town who are on different shows, and this one really allows us to supervise our words up on to the screen. For staff writers, that's unheard of. They're very free, and they believe in the imagination and autonomy of the writer, which is something you just don't find too often.

Q:

I thought your episode, "Nor Iron Bars Make a Cage," was a really good one.

A:

Interestingly, that was a Perlman idea. Ron had the germ of an idea that Vincent is discovered above ground with Cathy, and on that idea Alex and I ran with it. It turned into a very classical model; a Faustian kind of thing. We had this has-been professor whose work as a graduate student was stolen, and for twenty years he's been putzing around and sort of living on the fringe in this make-believe university in New York, studying the nocturnal habits of owls and whatever the hell he's doing. Then, while in Central Park, he spots Vincent, and he takes some fuzzy photographs. His superiors say, "You're crazy, this is nothing." Anyway, at the same time, Vincent is heart-broken because Catherine has decided that the relationship is preventing her from having a normal life in New York. She's really unhappy and gets this offer from the DA's office in Rhode Island, which would be a high profile, high pay, kind of position, and there's no way she can say no. So Vincent is heartbroken and careless, and in his carelessness, is in the upper world one evening when this professor and a young graduate student capture him. Then it becomes an exploration of what Vincent is. It's pretty standard and a very simple story, but it really was a chance for us to discuss Vincent's humanity. It was a low-budget, quickly-shot show. It was like a play, and came off very nicely.

Q:

To be honest, when I saw clips of the episode, I was reminded of another one where Vincent got trapped above. I was hoping this wouldn't become an oft-used theme.

A:

It's bad timing, as far as I'm concerned. That one was a really stylized show shot on the back lot. There was almost no dialogue, and in this one it's almost all dialogue. He's captured here, but this will be the last time you see him captured for quite a long time. The next one we did was "Song of Orpheus," which was kind of interesting. Roy Dotrice, who plays Father, was dealt with. There were a lot of flashbacks to the McCarthy era. We wanted to explore, again in an effort to find stories for these people and explain some of them as characters. You might ask, "Why is this educated man living underneath the streets of New York? Why is his name Father?" We actually trace the story that back in the Fifties he was a research physician for some fictional research institute, and he was commissioned to study the effects of nuclear fall-out—radiation. Back in the Fifties they glorified and extolled the atomic bomb, and to say other than that was viewed as the wrong thing to do, and anti-American. But he discovered that the radiation was fatal and for that he was blacklisted. At the same time, he was married to this New York socialite, and her father had the marriage annulled. So he lost his wife and his career at the same time, and he was down and out. Now that the woman is dying thirty five years later, he gets a message...she's not even sure if he's alive, but one of the helpers above brings word that she's dying. Father gets accused of murder and imprisoned, with Catherine and Vincent following his trail. Of course there's a happy ending where he finds Margaret and takes her down to the Underworld for the last week of her life. It's a real lyrical piece, and I think it came out nicely.

Q:

Okay, finally, if you had to reach the general public, what would you say to get them to watch **Beauty and the Beast**?

A:

That's a good question. First of all, do you want to see something you've never seen before on television? That's how I would preface it. And I'd say the show is full of heart, because of its emotional core. The premise doesn't do justice to what we actually see every week. To say that it's this beast that lives below the streets of Manhattan just has too many negative associations. Rather than try to give words to it, I'd say watch it. Experience it. And you'll see.

Episode Nine

"Dark Spirit"

Written by Robin Bernheim

Directed by Thomas J. Wright

At a black-tie dinner party, one of the guests begins to complain that it's hot in the room and that he feels like he's burning up. He picks up his glass and is stunned to see it filled with insects, which crawl out of it and onto his hands. He's suddenly on his feet in panic, imagining that the bugs are all over him. He runs around the room wildly, and ultimately plunges out the window, falling numerous stories to his death.

This sequence, as short as it is, seems awfully familiar, most notably from the feature film **Young Sherlock Holmes**, in which a hallucinogen was utilized to make people's imagination lead them to suicide. This year it was used again in one of the updated episodes of **Mission Impossible**. What began as an exciting story idea is becoming old hat awfully fast.

Next day, Catherine is talking to Joe Maxwell about the suicide which turns out to be murder. According to Joe, the butler, Hector Ocala, poisoned the man. The poison was found in the man's room, and the socialite had left the man fifty thousand dollars in his will. This seems to be enough proof for Catherine to investigate, and this appears to be an open-and-shut case. Joe doesn't agree, adding that the public defender has stated that Ocala is incompetent to stand trial, because the man claims to be a voodoo priest and has gone into a trance. Catherine is sent to check it out.

In prison she finds the man sitting cross-legged in his cell, chanting something, with the officer in attendance explaining that according to the public defenders, the man is casting a voodoo spell. Catherine leaves and goes to see Professor Ross, who is purportedly an authority on voodoo. She details the situation, and he explains that the man could be a voodoo priest, and *not* a murderer—he did, perhaps, put a spell on his victim. Ross goes on to explain some of the intricacies of voodoo magic, including ideas of possession and the like. "Voodoo long ago discovered a truth that modern medicine still resists," he says, "that the mind rules the body." If faith can heal, she muses, then fear can paralyze. Ross responds that it all depends on your point of view. He gives her a rock which he claims to be an important symbol in the voodoo world, and he suggests that she keep it for good luck. Then, when asked if Hector could be faking his trance, Ross says he would have to see the man before answering that question. Nodding, Catherine invites him to visit the "tombs."

We (very nicely) segue to the Underground tunnels, through which Vincent is slowly walking. Suddenly he is walking through a crowd of mourners. He stares down into an open casket with Catherine's body inside. Suddenly he awakens from his nightmare.

Catherine and Ross have arrived in prison where they stand before Hector's cell. The man suddenly slams himself against the door and continues his chanting, and claims of a beast being there. As they leave, Ross states that it is his belief that Hector's claim to be a voodoo priest is real. Later, Catherine goes to a voodoo shop, where she introduces herself to one Lindsey Gates, and starts to ask her about the murder. Hector, we learn, is actually a voodoo sorcerer, and his former employer was petrified of him. Catherine says the man was poisoned, but Lindsey points out that it wasn't poison which caused the man to leap to his death.

Joe Maxwell is astounded at Catherine's report, not believing the voodoo story at all. She goes back to the jail, and learns that Hector just dropped dead for no apparent reason. Returning home later that day, she discovers that her apartment has been ransacked, with her name written backwards on the wall—apparently in blood. There is a bloody image of the beast Hector spoke of; a beast that looks remarkably like Vincent. Then he is suddenly there, outside on the terrace. While being told that the police are on the way, Vincent replies that whoever did this was trying to frighten her. She refuses to be frightened.

Next day, Ross is over her apartment, explaining that the same thing was done to his home. He adds that Hector's followers will continue until his death is avenged, and that those people are intent on scaring her to death. He asks her for a dinner date, which she agrees to.

Father and Vincent are discussing voodoo. Vincent says he's going to speak to Narcissa, an elderly woman who truly believes in the world of voodoo. Father points out that she lives in a world of fantasy and spirits, which Vincent acknowledges. But if he's to save Catherine, then it is a world that he must visit.

Catherine talks to Hector's brother, who does not believe in voodoo and is hesitant to talk about it, until she threatens to involve the police. The man does reveal that Hector's boss was killed so that they could get to him and his power. He adds that they will kill her as well if she continues to ask questions.

Vincent goes to an area of the Underground that is quite majestic in its appearance. The wind is blowing fiercely, but he continues through the tunnels until he reaches the lair of Narcissa, the blind woman who nonetheless knows who he is. Vincent tells her the situation with Catherine. Moments later, she explains that they've put his friend under a curse, and the voodoo will work on someone who believes in fear.

Elsewhere, a voodoo chant is being performed. A photo of Catherine is placed in a bowl, as is a large snake. Meanwhile, Catherine leaves work and heads for her car in the garage. She starts driving and screeches to a halt when she feels a snake wrapping itself around her leg. She throws it out of the vehicle and stares at it in *fear* . At dinner that night with Ross, she notes that she doesn't believe in voodoo, but she is terrified of snakes. Ross explains that his investigation revealed that Hector was actually advising wall street financiers on the investments they should make. When Catherine adds that she doesn't believe in curses, Ross says, "if you believe magic can kill, then it can." She asks about the drawing on her wall, and he explains that it is the face of the demon that will destroy her. Naturally this upsets her slightly, despite his statement that if she doesn't believe, then nothing will happen. Suddenly she's feeling very hot.

We go back to the lair of the person responsible for the snake in Catherine's car, and see her picture being placed in the bowl again. The camera pulls back and we see that it is actually Ross, who is delivering a voodoo chant. Lindsey is there with him. Ross prays to his gods for aid in destroying their enemies.

Catherine awakens at home to find her bed swarming with spiders. She screams out and backs away, swatting them to the floor with her pillow. She is terrified. Vincent senses her fear in the Underground.

Next morning, Ross arrives at Catherine's apartment and tries to console her (and it's important to note how unsettling it is to *know* that Ross is behind this, and yet to witness his playing best friend to Catherine. This is a really effective idea that plays very nicely). Ross prepares tea for her, and pours a powder into her cup. She drinks the tea. Moments later she starts getting drowsy. He massages her neck until she falls asleep. Catherine awakens some time later, claiming that she really does feel better. Ross kisses her good-bye, while Catherine has the look of someone drugged (which, of course, she is). Picking up the tea cup, she also picks up the rock Ross had given her earlier.

Catherine goes to tell Joe what happened with the spiders, but he refuses to believe her. Joe wants to put her on another case. She is then terrified to see blood beginning to flow out from a pile of papers on Joe's desk. He, of course, doesn't see it. Catherine closes her eyes for a moment, and when she reopens them the blood is gone. He moves towards her to help, but she runs out screaming when it looks like his hands are covered with blood. In the ladies room, she looks in the mirror and sees scars on her face, which bring back the image from the pilot after her attack by the punks. Moving back to her desk she tries calling Ross, but is terrified to find that he's not at work. Edie comes over to offer help as does Joe. Catherine claims that she's merely tired. He suggests that she take the rest of the day off. As she pushes her way through the people working in the office she screams out when one of them appears to be a walking corpse.

Catherine goes home. The images continue as she stares into the bathroom mirror and sees even more scars on her face. There is a tapping on the terrace doors. Still grasping the stone given to her by Ross, she sees Vincent, and cries out that she doesn't know what's happening. Vincent says it isn't real, that everything she's experiencing is in her mind. Catherine looks at her hands to see that they're covered in blisters and boils. He wants to help her, but Catherine claims that he's the one doing this to her and that she doesn't even know who he is. She starts to back away, shouting out something about the image on her wall; that the image is him. She moves closer to the edge of the terrace.

"Catherine!" he shouts, and it is truly a powerful moment to see Vincent sounding anything but gentle. "You are my life. How can I help you?"

She responds that he should never come back and that she hates him. Now in the course of the series we've seen Vincent clawed open, burned, surviving an explosion and being hit by a car, but nothing he's been through has pained him to the extent that these words do. This despite the fact he knows it's not Catherine speaking of her own free will. Moving inside, Catherine picks up the phone, calls Ross and begs him to help her.

Ross is at home, awaiting Catherine's arrival, when he is visited by Lindsey. He tells her that this is not the time to lose her faith because they're so close to accomplishing their objective. They prepare for a voodoo ceremony.

In the Underground, Narcissa tells Vincent that Catherine is being affected by a drug, and that she will die. Vincent wants to go to her, but Narcissa says that the evil one will take away his soul. "He preys on weakness," Vincent replies sternly. "He has no power."

Ross is chanting a prayer for strength to strike out at their enemies. Moments later, Catherine, looking quite ragged, arrives. He offers her a potion to drink. Catching sight of her photo amongst those of Hector and his employer, she realizes what's going on and refuses to drink. Ross tries to force her and manages to get some in her. She falls to the floor half conscious. Ross picks up a knife, stares at the bloody image of the beast, and is about to stab her, when Vincent suddenly drops through the skylight, howling. Ross is actually delighted, stretching his arms out and dropping items which start a fire that spreads rapidly. He moves in to embrace Vincent, but is swatted to the side. He picks up Catherine's body and starts to carry her out. Ross tries to walk through the fire to reach Vincent, but doesn't make it.

Days later, Catherine is back at work, talking to Joe and stating that she's feeling much better. They also discuss the fact that Lindsey poisoned Hector's employer and are both amazed at Ross' involvement.

That night, Catherine is fondling the sacred stone on her terrace. Vincent is suddenly there. They look into each other's eyes as Vincent grabs the stone, crushes it to dust and throws it into the air. Catherine places her face gently on his chest.

The first thing that should be noted is that Linda Hamilton does a great job in this episode as Catherine at her most maddened. She gives a performance which rivals Sally Field's portrayal in **Sybill**.

While this is an effective enough episode, it really does seem somewhat out of place with the rest of the series, perhaps because of this strange mixture of genres. **Beauty and the Beast** has already proved itself quite capable of mixing the reality of Catherine and New York with the fantasy of Vincent and the Underworld. Adding an element of the supernatural just might be asking a little too much of the audience because it takes them out of the reality they've already accepted. One can only assume that this is the reason that Vincent plays a relatively small part in this episode.

Episode Ten

"A Children's Story"

Written by B.I. Barnett

Directed by Gabrielle Beaumont

Two children make their way through the streets of New York. One, looking something like a vagabond, is preparing to get on a skate board, while another is running away from two men in panic. The two children start running together and hide from the men. While they're hiding in an alleyway, the kid who was running admits that he escaped from a foster home, one from which children have a habit of disappearing. When he thinks he's safe, that kid moves into the open, saying that he's staying "far away from Ridley." No sooner have the words left his lips then the two men grab him and carry him away.

Vincent and Father discuss a new passageway for the tunnels which is currently being built, when Kipper, the vagabond-like child we met earlier, comes in, apologizing for being late for his lesson. Vincent senses that something is bothering the boy, and he details what happened on the surface and that he wishes he could have brought the boy down to the Underworld.

Catherine comes home that evening and steps out onto the terrace, where she finds a rose and a note from Vincent, asking her to meet him in the tunnels. He arrives, and we learn that it's supposedly been quite some time since they've seen each other (although we're never told why). They spend a moment discussing how seeing each other brings great joy, coupled with a deeply felt pain for the life that can never be. While they talk, they are separated by a steel grate which seals off the tunnel, symbolic, no doubt, of the barrier that exists between them. When asked what they can do, Vincent replies that all they can do is try to endure the pain as best they can. He opens the door, and nears Catherine. While all this works, the symbolism is a bit obvious, and the dialogue, as touching as it is, seems to come out of left field when considering the pace that the episode was building concerning the kid on the surface.

Getting to the subject at hand, Vincent notes Ridley Hall, which Catherine says is supposed to be a very good Foster home. He disagrees, stating that children are being hurt in that home, and there is no one to protect them. She promises to look into the situation right away.

Joe Maxwell and Catherine are debating the situation, with the former noting that he is juggling seven cases at one time which are all getting ready to go to trial. Catherine points out that they're talking about children. He agrees, telling her to make it fast. Before Catherine leaves the office, he notes that an undercover cop friend of his saw her walking through the park on the previous night, and he wants to know if she's lost her mind. Catherine replies that she was just out for some fresh air.

Catherine goes to Ridley's, where she meets the head of the institute, Richard Barnes. He seems very happy to help her, and begins a tour. She notes how well behaved the children are, and is given permission to go off on her own to speak to some of the kids. One of the men we had seen earlier walks by, dressed in a maintenance uniform, and is told to keep an eye on her. Catherine, meanwhile, goes to a recreation room where she starts talking to a little girl, but the child, who seems very frightened, says that she's not supposed to talk to strangers. Catherine leaves the room, and encounters a small boy who instantly says that Peter didn't run away, "they took him." Just as he identifies himself as Eric, his sister grabs him by the hand and hauls him away.

Going back to work, she wants to take Eric out of there so she can talk to him away from the building, and makes arrangements to pick him up the next morning. Later that evening she double-dates at the opera, but she doesn't seem to like her date, Greg, very much. There's no chemistry. At home, she steps onto the terrace and stares into the city. Vincent sits in his chamber, alone.

The next day, Catherine goes to see Barnes, who cheerfully greets her. She presents the transfer order for Eric, who she verbally identifies as having a sister in the home as well. Barnes explains that both children ran away the night before. It's obvious that Catherine doesn't believe him at all. She calls Children's Social Services to verify that the missing status of the children has been reported. When told that it has, she informs Barnes that she'll be back. As soon as Catherine leaves, Barnes goes into a locked room where Eric awaits him, and states that the boy is going to be transferred. Eric wants to know where his sister is and is told that she's being transferred as well. Barnes violently hauls him out of the room, and the two punks seen earlier are pulling his sister out of the house. They bring her to a basement where there are a large group of other kids who have all been "sentenced" to this place. Frankly, it seems to represent conditions worse than a transient hotel. In another building, Eric sits in a very small room, all alone.

Catherine has Edie try to tap into Ridley's computer, but access is denied. While she continues trying, Catherine makes her way through the streets of New York and sadly takes in all the homeless children and people, begging for some money just to make it through another day. That night she steps back onto the terrace at home, where Vincent is awaiting her. Crying, she tells him that she feels as though she's done more harm than good. "Those who prey on children steal everybody's hope," says Vincent. "Don't give up hope."

At work the next day, Edie and Catherine go to Children's Social Services where they secretly go through the file room. Despite it being lunch time, a worker is still there. Edie tries to distract him with flirting, while Catherine gets the file she needs and departs. Taking note of this, Edie breaks off her conversation.

In the streets, we see a group of kids from the basement home (for wont of a better name) working together to pickpocket an elderly man. One of the punks is explaining this to Ellie (Eric's sister) so that she'll know what will eventually be expected of her.

From the stolen file, Catherine and Edie learn that the kids were taken to the Foster facility. Meanwhile, Barnes is meeting with one of the punks, who hands him an envelope with fifteen hundred dollars in it. Barnes says he wanted twenty five hundred, and that this is the last kid he's delivering. It's becoming too risky to keep supplying him with children. Vincent, we learn, has been watching from a wooded area.

Catherine goes to the Foster facility, where one of the children tells her that the "new kid" is locked up in detention. She makes her way up the stairs and to the detention room. Tapping on the door she calls out to Eric. A woman in charge comes up behind her and tries to pull Catherine away from the door, but Catherine is easily able to push her away while grabbing the keys to the room. Eric gets out, and is told to get in the car up front. Catherine locks the woman in the detention room and starts to follow him (why would she send the kid ahead without her? It just doesn't make sense). She heads for the stairs when one of the punks tries to grab her, but she throws him down the stairs and runs by his body. She and Eric are in her car, and drive off.

Kipper comes to Vincent in the underground, and informs him that Catherine is waiting for him at the entrance to the tunnel. He goes to her and finds Catherine with the sleeping form of Eric. She goes on to explain that the boy was separated from his sister and she has to go and get her, but what about Eric? Vincent considers this and adds that the boy will be safe with them. She awakens the child, who is stunned at Vincent's appearance. He touches his face, and asks him how he got to look the way he does.

"I don't know," Vincent replies simply. "And I don't think I ever will. I never knew my mother and father."

This is a nice moment, representing a "meeting of minds," if you will between Vincent and Eric, who have a common background in that they're both orphans. It's also interesting to see how quickly the boy accepts Vincent for what he is, when an adult would no doubt react in fear.

The punk is in his basement establishment, teaching the children how to steal. Ellie says she won't participate, but another girl confidently says she will. Back Underground, Eric is talking to Father who tells the boy that he's welcome to stay with them if he wants to, until Catherine can find a place for them. He also adds that there are promises that have to be made, such as his being willing to provide help and support to those who need it, and to accept it from those who offer it. Eric agrees, saying that he would promise not to tell anybody about this place. Father appreciates this.

Back above, Ellie is yelled at for screwing up in her pickpocketing a mannequin.

Underground Vincent tucks Eric in, reinforcing the idea that he's safe and with friends.

The punk approaches Ellie and says, "I own you. I bought you. Without me you got the chickenhawks on the street. You wanna be selling your body?" Ellie cries that she doesn't want to be there either, and the punk starts to beat her up.

In her office, Catherine is told by Joe that they're going to get Ridley on child abuse charges. Naturally she's delighted.

In the Underground, Vincent shows a photo of the punk which several of the children recognize from the Times Square area. Eric looks at the photo and says that he's the guy who took his sister. Kipper is asked to find the man, see where he lives and report. Kipper returns to the surface, and in a montage of shots, eventually locates the punk leading a group of the kids to where they live. This information is conveyed to Catherine, who goes underground and meets Vincent. He leads her through the tunnels to the area where the building is, and Catherine ends up in the basement through a hidden panel that Vincent knew about. She grabs Ellie and starts making her way out, when the punk approaches and tries to stop them. Without another word, Catherine kicks him in the shin and punches him in the face. As he goes down, she grabs Ellie by the hand and starts running away. He manages to get back to his feet and calls out for one of his men. That guy starts running, but Vincent reaches out from a drainage duct on the floor and hauls the man within. The punk, furious, runs through the basement, and right into Vincent, who claws him and whips him out of frame.

Later, the employees of Ridley are arrested. Meanwhile, Ellie is brought to the Underground, where she is reunited with Eric. "It's a dream," says Ellie of this place. "No," Eric counters. "It's better."

Catherine and Vincent are alone, with her admitting that she's never felt as complete as she does at this moment. Vincent says he can feel the sensation she's experiencing.

"It's like a dream," says Catherine.

"No," Vincent adds, mirroring the words of the children a moment earlier. "It's better."

"A Children's Story" is probably the first episode of **Beauty and the Beast** which isn't satisfying. While the sentiment behind the story is valid, the execution as presented doesn't gel. The scenes between Catherine and Vincent in which they discuss their relationship almost seem gratuitous, and not very believable, which is particularly disappointing when considering that the relationship is the core of the series.

For some reason the story of the children doesn't come across as completely believable. Yes the punks are scum, but we don't get to see the children in enough danger. The methods in which the villains of the piece are disposed of does not provide the catharsis that a tale of child abuse should. This is an important issue which simply must be handled delicately. Unfortunately, this script just didn't do it.

A final thought: it's great that Ellie and Eric are being allowed to live in the Underground, but what about the rest of the children? What happens to them?

Episode Eleven

"An Impossible Silence"

Taped

Written by Howard Gordon and Alex Ganza

Directed by Christopher Leitch

A cop named Perotta is talking to a man named Yates, and is in the midst of saying goodnight. Perotta gets in his car, while Yates discreetly pulls out a pistol and shoots the man at point blank range. A mute teenager from the Underground has seen everything and begins to run in fear. Yates catches sight of her and starts in pursuit. Through sheer luck and determination, she manages to elude bullet shots until a wino runs into the arms of a police officer. Yates has no choice but to pull back.

Vincent is talking to someone in the Underground, when Laura runs crying into his arms, pointing behind her. In the DA's office the next day, Joe Maxwell is telling how frustrating it is to meet with the press regarding the murder of a cop, but by the same token he could do worse for his career than putting away a cop killer. Standing before the press, Joe explains that a man named Curtis Jackson was arrested for the murder of Officer Perotta. Despite protests from the people in the room, he is not at liberty to discuss the situation any further, beyond stating that they are hoping to move quickly through a trial.

Elsewhere in the city, Yates is playing pool with two other men who argue back and forth whether killing Perotta was a good idea, but the bottom line is that the cop would have blown their drug operation, which nets upwards of one hundred thousand dollars per month. Jackson, they are proud to point out, is the one going to fry for the crime, leaving them untouched.

In the Underground, Laura and Vincent are talking via sign language, with her pointing to a newspaper story on the murder and making it clear that Jackson is *not* the man who murdered the police officer. Vincent then realizes that she actually saw the killer, and that he was a white man, not black as Jackson is. He tries to console her, promising that he will help.

That night, Catherine goes to the park and enters a tunnel. Meeting with Vincent, who explains that Laura was an abandoned child (probably abandoned by her parents who wanted a "normal" child) brought Underground by a helper. He moves to the subject at hand, stating that according to Laura, Jackson was not the man who murdered the police officer. Catherine finds this a little difficult to accept, as the evidence found against the man is considered nothing less than overwhelming. Vincent is quick to add that Laura is aware of what her statement means: she might have to go up to the surface to testify. Catherine says that she will do everything in her power to prevent that from happening, but their options seem very limited. Later, still in the underground, Laura feels the vibrations made by the clanging pipes around her, and a look of great joy crosses her face.

Vincent and Father discuss what is happening, with the latter thinking she should not go above. Vincent believes the time will come when she will need to grow beyond all they can offer, and right now that need must be fulfilled in the trial which will free an innocent man, and hopefully convict the guilty one. While Father states that the problem is not theirs to worry about, Vincent responds that neither is the decision. As he goes off to find her, the camera holds on Father's face.

While the opening sequence of this episode is really quite similar to those of "A Children's Story," "An Impossible Silence" is already working much better. Laura's situation seems a much more pressing one, and a much greater dilemma for the individual. Also important to note is Father's reaction to her possibly going to the surface. From what we have gathered so far in the course of the series, it would seem that as progressive as he would like to be, he is a man deeply frightened by the surface world and what it represents. We've seen it first with his reaction to the relationship between Vincent and Catherine, his own return to that realm in "Song of Orpheus" and now in this story. Reading into this, perhaps he is a man extremely comfortable in this world he has helped wrought, and maybe he's just afraid of people leaving him alone down there. If this is true, it adds a fascinating layer of paranoia to the character.

Catherine is meeting with Jackson at the police station, and he is naturally suspicious at her wanting to help him get out. At the outset of their conversation all he can do is make jokes about his reputation. Catherine is not amused, stating that she's fully aware of his drug-dealing history, and that if she had her way she would "bury" him. This seems to be enough to pull him out of his giddy mood. She adds that she doesn't believe he's the one responsible for the cop's death, but she expects him to help her find out who killed the cop. They discuss the fact that he had once threatened Perotta when the cop had busted him, but that it was nothing more than an empty threat. The gun found in his car? Somebody put it there. Catherine wants to know who.

Later, she meets with Detective Keller, who turns out to be one of the men we had seen earlier with Yates, who, as the scene goes on, we also learn is a cop. When Keller explains that they're grateful for the DA's office putting Jackson away so quickly, Catherine replies that they don't believe he killed the officer, and that there is an eyewitness to the crime. Keller doesn't want to hear this, stating that Jackson is the man. A moment later he calms down and apologizes for the outburst. She asks for his cooperation in giving her a place to start, and he says he'll have his thoughts together in a few minutes.

Vincent and Father talk to Laura in sign language, emphasizing that the decision must be that of the woman's. She wants to know if she can come back should she leave, and they respond in the affirmative. Laura turns to Vincent for advice, but he points out that it is not his place to make her decision for her. His only suggestion is that she follow her heart. A moment later, the decision is made: she will go above.

Although the synopsis cannot do it justice, this is really a beautiful sequence, as we watch these three people communicate with each other via sign language. Taking a cue from **Children of a Lesser God**, director Christopher Leitch and writers Howard Gordon and Alex Ganza, as well as the cast members, have delivered a truly viable dramatic sequence with very little dialogue. A nice job by all.

In the DA's office, Joe is furious at Catherine for investigating the crime behind his back. They go into his office where she tells him that there was a witness to the crime. Can she produce the witness? She says not as of yet, which sets him off again. It's his feeling that they have in their hands an open-and-shut cop killer case, and her actions may be the ones which are ruining it. Catherine argues for the man's *possible* innocence, but Joe suggests that she leave it alone. She responds that there may be a hidden agenda here, that the truth could make for an embarrassing press conference. Joe counters by stating that his father was a cop who had his throat slashed by two punks who had just robbed him, and they let the man bleed to death. No arrest. No trial. "They were fourteen years old," he says as he leaves the office, "and so was I." This touches Catherine deeply, but the man is gone without another word.

Not to belabor the point, but again we're presented with another dramatically sound sequence. It helps to develop the characters a little more deeply and keeps the story moving at a steady pace.

Laura gathers the things she will need for her journey to the surface, obviously torn at leaving the Underground, but perhaps realizing that this is the beginning of a new life for her. As she looks at and touches the various objects in her dwelling, we see the young woman getting ready to leave the little girl behind. Looking into a mirror, she tries to speak, but only the slightest of sounds come forth.

When Catherine returns home that night, Yates and his partner are waiting for her, wearing stockings over their heads. They slap her around quite a bit, stating that "The only thing worse than a cop killer, is someone who covers up for one." They warn her to back off, deliver some vicious punches and kicks and depart. Shortly thereafter, Vincent arrives, enters through the terrace doors and carries her to the bedroom, where he tends to her lovingly. He gets ready to leave, but she asks him not to, saying that she needs him close to her. "I'll watch over you," he says as she falls to sleep. He moves to the corner of the room, and does just that.

The next day, Vincent leads Laura out of the tunnel, where Catherine is waiting for her. Vincent promises that he will be watching over her. Laura thanks him, but he tells her that she should thank herself, for having the courage to do what she's doing, and seeing that there is life beyond the tunnels.

That night, Laura is at Catherine's apartment, and Catherine explains to her that the deposition is going to be rough because lawyers "aren't always very nice." Laura motions to the bruises on Catherine's face and asks why they happened to her. The reason is simple enough: no one except Catherine wants her on this case, and this was the way they tried to deliver their message.

Next day at police headquarters, several police officers and an interpreter are in the interrogation room, along with Joe Maxwell. Laura, via sign language, details what she saw, including the fact that Perotta was killed inside his car. This convinces everyone that this is the "real thing" as that fact hasn't been released to the public as of yet. After the interrogation, and after Laura has done a superb job of describing the events she witnessed, the two of them are enroute out of the building when Catherine is informed that there is a phone call for her from the DA's office. She sits Laura down in a waiting area and goes for the call. While she's gone, Yates begins to approach Laura, who recognizes him as the guilty man. He stands right in front of her, and she tries to move away, only to be stopped by the man's partner. They pull her away, just a moment before Catherine approaches the waiting area, alarmed to find Laura missing. She moves outside, but the girl is no where to be seen.

No matter how much praise has been given to this episode thus far, it's really annoying that such a story contrivance would be allowed to take place. It's a transparent, and fairly lame, excuse used to separate Catherine and Laura. Right from the moment she's told that there's a phone call for her, you just know what's going to happen next.

Catherine goes to the Underground in tears, not knowing what she should do. Vincent wants to know if she's called the police, but the police have no idea where to start looking. Catherine says that the girl could be anywhere; she could be dead. Vincent doesn't even want to consider that possibility. Communication over the "pipeline" alerts them to the fact that a message is being delivered. The camera cuts to the hideout of Yates and the others, where Laura is handcuffed, and tapping a message into the pipes she is attached to. Naturally they don't suspect that she's up to anything. The tapping finally gets on their nerves, and they stop her. Moments later she starts again.

Yates is loading his gun, saying that this is the time to tie up loose ends. Keller doesn't want to hear of it, comparing Laura's age to that of his daughter's.

Underground communication has revealed that Laura is being held in Brooklyn. Vincent is off like a flash. Back in the hideout (Keller's home), Keller and Yates are virtually at each other's throat, with the former saying that he won't be involved in a young girl's murder. We cut to a subway car, where Vincent is travelling via his favorite means: on top of the train.

Keller gets ready to leave his home, and is nearly shot by Yates. He's held back by the third partner. Yates nears Laura, the gun in his hand. Suddenly the lights go out in the room. They see a shadow moving outside the basement window and assume it's Keller. They move away from Laura and begin searching for the man. Using a flashlight, Yates moves back towards Laura, and then above him to see the snarling face of Vincent, who leaps down and breaks the man's back. Before he falls lifelessly to the ground, a bullet accidentally goes off, striking the third partner, killing him instantly. Vincent bends down to gently free Laura.

Back at the DA's office the next day, Joe pulls Catherine into his office and apologizes for his attitude towards her, and for letting the situation get "personal." Of course she accepts his apology. Then he adds that Jackson will be set free that day, and that they discovered evidence which convicted all the dead cops and Keller as being on the take, and operating in the drug business.

That night at Catherine's apartment, Vincent is explaining that Father is upset that Laura is planning on moving to the surface world. He, too, is saddened, but he accepts it as inevitable. He believes that her strength is her vulnerability, which could be dangerous. Catherine believes that the young woman is going to be just fine. "She had a great teacher," Catherine smiles.

A truly excellent episode, and certainly a refreshing rebound from the disappointment of "A Children's Story." Everything from the acting to the writing to the directing is right on the mark.

Episode Twelve

"Shades of Grey"

Written by George R.R. Martin & David Peckinpah

Directed by Thomas J. Wright

Father is confronting a teenager named Mouse with the accusation that he's been stealing from the surface. The boy doesn't see it as stealing, because it's things they needed. He thinks their complaints are nonsense, as he points out that everyone takes things from "on top. That's what the top is there for." Father disagrees, pointing out that it's true they pick up things discarded from the people above, or accept things offered to them, but they do not steal.

Mouse says he needed elevator cables and hydraulics for a big project, which no one knew anything about. A teenaged girl explains that an iron ladder near the pipe chamber was rusted, and she had asked the boy to rig something to make the climb easier. Father doesn't see this as a good reason. He asks for a vote as to whether "the punishment" should be evoked, as this is just the latest of Mouse's robberies from the surface. The vote takes place with the numerous people around the boy turning their back to him. The sentence is passed: for one month, no one will speak to Mouse, because if their words have no affect on him, then perhaps their silence will. This doesn't bother Mouse, until he sees it in effect. Even Vincent will not speak to him, which pains him greatly.

This is a fascinating glimpse into the societal structure of the Underworld, providing us a glimpse of the "government" at work. While the punishment dealt out to Mouse may seem rather childish, its effect is quite profound. Like the Japanese who have disgraced their families, he is "dead" in their eyes until honor has been restored, which, in this case, will happen in one month's time.

Catherine goes into Joe's office, and he explains that Max Avery is "as dirty as they come." He has had building developers paying him off to keep their buildings going, but none of them will speak of it. The only developer who *is* willing to talk is Elliot Burch, who we last saw in "Siege." The catch is that he'll only talk to Catherine. Naturally she is outraged by this, but Joe points out that with his testimony, they could put Avery away forever.

In a home-made laboratory, Mouse is working on something, and talking to himself, complaining about the punishment the Underground has given him. Elsewhere, Father is looking through a kaleidescope, which was made for him by Mouse. Vincent approaches him, and they talk about the boy. Vincent admits that the sentence does bother him, but Father feels that it's better to do this, than to have to face prison above (as he did in "Song of Orpheus") and that this could happen if the thefts continued. At that moment, Ellie runs in saying that her brother Eric fell in the Maze (and the inclusion of these two children is a very nice touch of continuity from episode number ten, "A Children's Tale"). She leads Vincent and Father to him.

Catherine meets with Burch in his office. He's delighted to see her, but can tell that she's not happy being there. Elliot wants to know what he did to make her hate him so much, but she's confident that they both know the answer to that question.

Vincent and Father move into an area of the Maze, which is completely water saturated. Back in Burch's office, he has pulled out a file which details every threat, kickback and such that has involved Max Avery, and adds that it's enough to put the man away for at least two decades. Catherine reaches over for the file, but he holds it back for a moment. He tries to explain that he has dealt with a dozen Avery's in his life, because it allowed him to build his business to the extent it has grown. And yes his people were operating under his name (for full details see the "Siege" synopsis), but he swears that he didn't know the full extent of what was going on...maybe he didn't want to know. "I have a lot of regrets in my life," he says sincerely, "and losing you is one of them." As he pushes the file over to Catherine, he says that his attorney advised him to shred the material, so he got a new attorney. Catherine, trying not to let this conversation melt down the defenses she has built around her heart, states that by doing this, he's opening himself up to an onslaught of attacks by Avery. Burch believes that when it's all over, both New York and he will be rid of the man. This does seem to touch her.

Father and Vincent reach the area where Eric is. Suddenly the saturated ground begins to shake, rocks start to fall, and part of the wall gives away, causing Father and Vincent to be trapped beneath tons of rock. While both have lived, Vincent can only make out various shades of grey surrounding them, while Father is for all intents and purposes, completely blind.

Delivering the file to Joe, Catherine feels that for all he's doing, and for all that it will ultimately cost him, Elliot Burch should be granted immunity. Joe is a little surprised to hear her say this as it's a direct contradiction to what she was saying earlier. She points out that he's doing the right thing, and that should count for something. Joe thinks that immunity for Burch is a small price to pay to put Avery away.

The people from the Underground have gathered around the sealed off cavern, trying desperately to think of a way to get through to them. Winslow sends Kipper back to find all the maps in Father's chambers to see if there's another entrance to the tunnel. Winslow picks up a pick, and starts slamming it against the stone. "There's only one way to get through," he says. "One foot at a time."

Sitting at her desk, Catherine grabs her head suddenly, instinctively knowing that something has happened to Vincent.

Vincent is consoling Father, and states that he can hear someone pounding against the rock. Vincent insists that the man stay awake, as he may have a concussion, so the men start chatting away.

Everyone is trying to cut in, when a girl named Jamie says they should break the vow of silence and talk to Mouse, who may be able to rig something that will free the two of them. Winslow will hear none of it, believing that the boy will only get in the way. Elsewhere, Catherine has entered the tunnels and is searching slowly for everyone. She eventually finds Mouse, and pleads for his help. After a moment's hesitation, he agrees. As they move through the tunnels, Jamie arrives and tells them what's happened. Soon thereafter they arrive, and Mouse tells them that Father and Vincent will run out of air before they can get through. They'll have to find the other entrance he knows about. Winslow shows him the maps, pointing out that there is no other entrance. "Maps are wrong," snaps Mouse. "I know what I know." Mouse is shoved away by Winslow, so the boy goes off on his own, followed by many of the others. We hold on Winslow's look.

Here is a sample of jealousy, as Winslow seems to want to be in charge and would appear to have a need to be a hero. Mouse is a threat to that desire, so he has closed his mind off to any of the boy's suggestions, despite the fact that it may cost the lives of Father and Vincent. This just serves as proof that not everyone who has come from the surface has overcome their basic human drives and need to compete.

Vincent tells Father that he can feel Catherine near, crediting that to their bond, learning it must be stronger than he ever imagined. "It's as though your destinies were inextricably linked," muses Father. Then he reflects on the past, remembering a woman he had seen some forty years earlier, who was, in his mind, the most beautiful he had ever seen. Before he had a chance to speak to her, however, she got into a cab and was gone. A year later, he saw her getting out of a cab on the same street corner, and a year later they were married (for full details see the "Song of Orpheus" synopsis). He adds that he understands the relationship between Vincent and Catherine, as well as their bond. He, too, believes in miracles.

Mouse leads Catherine and two others to his work area, and shows them the drill device that they'll have to put together. They bring the equipment to the proper area and start putting it together, while we intercut between them and Winslow's rescue operation. They seem to be accepting the fact that they're not going to make it through in time to rescue Father and Vincent. Mouse's confidence is soaring, but then the drill breaks three inches in to the cutting. Angry, he says he's going to have to go to the surface to see if he can get the proper equipment, but he's worried about the time factor. Catherine considers this for a moment, mentions that there's someone she can speak to, and asks Mouse to guide her out of the tunnels.

She arrives at Elliot Burch's house, asking for his help. Catherine hands him a list of items she needs, and he jokingly asks her if she's giving up law for the mining business. Catherine snaps at him, claiming that she doesn't have time for his chatter (which wouldn't exactly incline most people to be willing to offer their resources). While she won't explain what she needs the equipment for, Catherine says that all she's asking is for Elliot to trust her. He half-laughs, stating that that's all he's ever asked of her. He starts dialing the phone, noting that he must have tried calling her fifty times and never once got a response. He contacts a foreman and tells him to give Catherine whatever she needs. She starts out of the house, then turns to him and says that the next time he calls, she'll be there. He wants to know why. "Because you didn't put a price tag on this," is her response.

Father is barely conscious. Vincent is doing his best to keep the man's thoughts lucid. Father states that their world must continue because many people depend on it, and if he doesn't make it, then it will be Vincent's voice that will be listened to. He forces Vincent to promise that the dream will be kept alive.

Catherine has rejoined Mouse with the equipment, and they move back into the Maze area. Within their "cell," Vincent feels that Catherine has returned, bringing hope with her. From outside, Mouse has begun the drilling process, but fears that it won't work. Catherine goes to Winslow and the others, and the man reluctantly agrees to join the other rescue area. Managing to get through one section of stone, they reach the next and Mouse lays plastic explosives on the rock. Then he sheepishly admits that he's never used explosives before, and while he may kill Father and Vincent, he may also save them. The results could go either way. Mouse says that he is the one who will trigger the explosives, even though he too may die in the process. Catherine, Winslow and everyone else begin to move away from the area.

The explosion is triggered, with the result being that everyone survives, although Father is in fairly bad shape. Winslow hoists Mouse to his feet and embraces him warmly. Later, Catherine and Vincent move through the tunnels alone, expressing the love they feel for each other. They move towards what looks to be their first kiss, but then they merely embrace, thus allowing **Beauty and the Beast** to join such series as **Who's the Boss** and **Moonlighting**, filling the audience with one question: when are the two leads going to take the...shall we say...plunge?

What can one say? Another terrific episode, delving into the highly original characters and providing insight as to what makes them tick. The premise of a cave-in trapping two characters and allowing them the opportunity to express their feelings, fears and dreams to each other, was done to good success in the short-lived **Planet of the Apes** TV series of the mid-1970s, and only moderately well in the "Arsenal of Freedom" episode of **Star Trek: The Next Generation.** It is here, however, that the story premise is explored to its fullest potential. We are, however, left with one dangling question: what becomes of Elliot Burch? Will he become a recurring theme during the second season, or be dropped completely?

Episode Thirteen

"China Moon"

Written by Cynthia Benjamin

Directed by Christopher Leitch

Vincent is in the midst of reading, when he hears from the annual Chinese New Year Parade above. Music is being played, fireworks exploded, and so on. He listens intently, taking it all in, perhaps wishing that he could partake in the festivities.

A Chinese man is congratulating his grandson (Peter Chang) and his fiance (Lin Wan), welcoming her to the family and stating that the intermixing of their bloodlines should result in an extraordinary grandchild. From the woman's facial expression, we can tell that she's not pleased with the current situation, and has only agreed to get married to uphold her family's tradition.

Elsewhere, another man (Henry) is being beaten up quite severely in his restaurant, and told that he should find himself a new girlfriend. The two attackers knock him into unconsciousness and then depart. Vincent, in the meantime, has come to a shop to pick up special herbs for Father from a friend of the Underground.

Lin is being dropped off by her fiance, who had taken note of her less than happy attitude at dinner and tells her that she will do what she's told to, smile when she's supposed to smile and express the proper gratitude. The car drives off, and Henry comes running up to her, suggesting that the two of them escape from their families and "find a way to be together." They kiss, embrace and then go their separate ways. Lin goes to her grandfather's shop, and is not surprised at all to see Vincent. Apparently he's a good friend of the family.

On Catherine's terrace that night, Vincent is pondering the world's apparent conspiracy to keep lovers apart, with Catherine offering the alternative —bringing them together when it's impossible. Changing the subject, Vincent tells Catherine of the situation between Lin and Henry. She offers to talk to her, which he thinks would be a good idea.

The next day, Lin is talking to Catherine in her grandfather's shop, discussing the situation. The girl is torn between her loyalty to family and what her heart is telling her to do. Catherine can identify with this, comparing it to her father who essentially dominated her, making all her decisions, until the day finally came when she could stand up for herself, and began making her own decisions. "It took Vincent to show me that the truth is in your heart," Catherine notes. "And you should follow it."

Nothing would give Lin greater pleasure, but things aren't quite so simple for her. She is deeply in love with Henry, and is pained that he was beaten up the previous night. This catches Catherine by surprise, who says that she can help her do something about that. Lin refuses the offer, although she's grateful.

Henry is talking to one of his workers and a most valued friend (Eddie), when there is a noise outside the restaurant. He cautiously steps outside, and is surprised to find Lin waiting for him. She embraces and kisses him, and says that they're going to get away from this place. He wants to know what she's talking about, but her only response is for him to trust her. This place they are going to go to is a safe and comforting one, and they will meet at her grandfather's shop at nine o'clock the following night. They kiss passionately again, with Eddie standing within earshot of them, having overheard everything.

Later, Lin meets with Vincent, asking that the tunnels provide some sanctuary to her and Henry. Vincent is hesitant, pointing out that the rules are very strict insofar as allowing new people to move below, plus he is going to have to speak to her grandfather. She pleads her case further, and after a moment's hesitation, Vincent says that he will speak with Father and contact her when he knows something.

Underground, Vincent and Father are debating the situation, with Father arguing that they don't even know who this Henry is (Vincent argues that Lin does, and that's what's important), and that they would be going against her grandfather's wishes (which is countered by the statement that she is not the possession of any man), who they owe much to. He only wants what's best for Lin, says Father. "Only Lin knows what's best for Lin," Vincent replies. Father considers this for a moment and says he will present it to the Council. There isn't time for that. Another moment of silence, and then Father adds that he and Vincent will have to share the responsibility of their decision.

It's interesting to note that Vincent's argument here with Father harkens back to the premiere episode, in which he had to defend his decision to bring Catherine down to the tunnels in the first place so that she could heal. Vincent probably identifies completely with the Lin/Henry situation, and sees this solution as the only one to help love conquer impossible odds. If only there were such a solution for he and Catherine....

Catherine is meeting with Henry, explaining that if he identifies any of the men who assaulted him, then the DA's office can move in and do something about it. He would rather leave things alone, stating that Chinatown is a world of its own, and that she and the police are the outsiders. She gives him her card, saying she'll do anything to help if he wants her to. Catherine leaves the store. Henry approaches Eddie, discusses how badly business has been and states that he's going to have the store signed over to him, as they "grew up" in this place. Maybe with him gone, Chang's people will allow some customers in. Eddie wants to know where Henry is going, but he won't say, only stating that he'll be in touch as soon as he can.

From there, Henry meets with Lin and they are about to depart when Peter Chang and his men move in to surround them. Henry sends Lin off running, while he is slammed against a wall. Peter pulls out a knife and approaches him. Meanwhile, Lin runs down to a tunnel area to hide. Chang's men follow her into the basement of her grandfather's shop, but there's no sign of the woman. Meanwhile, Peter moves in to kill Henry, but the other man is fast, and manages to slam his attacker against a wall, accidentally causing Peter to stab himself at the same time.

Chang, the boy's grandfather, keeps his anger over his grandson's death under tight control, but he wants vengeance and sends his people out to find Henry. The next day, Henry is standing across the street from his restaurant, when he sees Eddie receiving a payoff from Chang's men. Deeply disturbed, he moves off. Going to a telephone booth, he calls Catherine and tells her exactly what's happened, and about Lin's "secret place," but admits he doesn't know where it is. Catherine considers this and tells him to meet her uptown. He leaves the phone booth, and is followed by a pair of Chang's men.

Catherine and Henry meet each other and are walking, and then running from Chang's men. She leads him into the basement of a building and into a secret tunnel entrance and a steel door that blocks their way. The two men are still following. Catherine taps on the door in a specific way, and a moment later Vincent opens it. Henry is stunned at Vincent's appearance, but nonetheless moves in. The door is closed behind them. The two men reach the "dead end," assume they must have gone the wrong way and leave.

In the Underground, Henry is reunited with Lin, finding it hard to believe that any of this strange world is real. "It's as real as your love," says Vincent. Then, Lin's grandfather comes down to describe the ramifications of what they've done. Vincent explains that the responsibility is all of theirs, but the man points out that Chang is aware of the tunnels, and that he'll undoubtedly send down a whole army to extract revenge. This is a nightmare come true for Father.

Chang, now dressed as a warrior, has gathered his army and is preparing to enter the tunnels. He hands out weapons of their ancestors (i.e. swords, Ninja stars, etc.), and they embark on their mission. Elsewhere, Father is preparing for the attack, making plans for the children to be moved to safety, false walls to be erected, the tapping on the pipes to stop, the lights to be shut off by Mouse, etc. Henry wants to turn himself over to them, stating that it's *his* fight. Vincent doesn't believe there will be a fight, and if there is, they shall fight back. This is, after all, their home being threatened, and they will do what they must to prove victorious.

Consulting a map, Chang sends several of his men one way, and leads the others through the tunnels. They manage to open the dead end door seen earlier, and start moving through it. Then the lights go out, but Chang's confidence remains strong.

Father informs everyone that both groups have made their way to the lower levels. They've been safe for so long, he muses, and now these people from above are going to bring their violence and their hatred to the Underground. Vincent prepares to leave, stating that if he's not back within an hour, they should all flee. Catherine grabs him before he leaves. "Come back to me," she whispers.

As one group makes its way through the tunnels, Vincent takes a tip from Rambo, disposing of the men one-by-one by seemingly appearing out of nowhere, dispatching someone and then disappearing into the mist again. Soon thereafter, Chang's group hears the low growling of Vincent, and then his scream of fury.

This is an effective scene, with everyone's voice and Vincent's growls echoing. Director Christopher Leitch conveys a great deal of suspense and atmosphere, making you believe that this Underground really does exist.

The group spreads out (don't these guys ever learn?) and, again, Vincent starts disposing of them one at a time. A member of this group, who has armed himself with a gun, is shooting blindly at every sound, accidentally killing one of his own men. Vincent rushes him, slams his body against a wall and kills the man. Then he turns his attention to Chang, who is armed with a Samurai sword. Chang looks at him, and calls Vincent a demon. "All men are demons when their home and loved ones are at risk," he says in response.

Chang drops his sword, saying that he will return again and again with his people better armed for each battle. He voices his opinion that Vincent will not kill an unarmed man, because that's the type of thing that only a "monster" would do. Vincent approaches him, apparently willing to prove him wrong, while behind him one of Chang's people has managed to get to his feet, and is armed with a Ninja star. The star is thrown, and Vincent ducks at the last possible second, causing the weapon to lodge in Chang's heart. The man falls lifelessly to the ground, as does the wounded "soldier" who threw the star. Vincent stands, and looks at the bodies around him in sadness.

Later, Henry and Lin are married in the Underground. During the ceremony, Catherine and Vincent stare at each other, both cognizant of how love has conquered impossible odds. Perhaps someday the same will be true for them.

By episode thirteen, **Beauty and the Beast** has only had one real disappointment, which is truly an amazing ratio. Few series are able to deliver so many consecutively good shows. Probably the strongest aspect of "China Moon" is its theme of undying love conquering impossible odds, and the comparison between the relationship of Lin and Henry with that of Catherine and Vincent. As happy as you are that the two lovers have found happiness by episode's end, you can't help but feel for the two leads, wondering if they will ever get a similar opportunity for happiness.

Episode Fourteen

"The Alchemist"

Story by Richard Setlowe, Teleplay by Alex Gansa &Howard Gordon

Directed by Thomas J. Wright

A woman sprinkles a powdery substance on herself, and is instantly plunged into a hallucinogenic state of mind. She starts laughing giddily, then looks down upon a fire hydrant, but sees it as a midget dressed as a fireman. Believing that this man must be very cold, she removes her wrap and places it on the hydrant. To her eyes, the midget hugs it tightly to himself, and smiles up at her lovingly. Still laughing, the woman steps into traffic and experiences a vision which can only be described as an electric light show through a ride at Disneyland. Then she is struck by a car.

Catherine is wired by Joe Maxwell and a SWAT captain. She's admittedly nervous at going undercover. Joe feels it is too dangerous, but Catherine points out that nobody twisted her arm to do this. She gets out of a van and walks into a nightclub. Elsewhere in the establishment, we see the bartender pushing a small packet of *something* across the bar and into the hands of a waiting patron. In a back room, two men are discussing a drug transaction, with Tyler Buckman, the owner of the club, stating that he needs more of "the stuff," because he's not meeting demands. The older man suggests he raise his prices, but the owner points out that he's already at a thousand dollars a gram. The man nonetheless makes his pay-off, stating that he wants to get more of the drug as soon as he can.

Elsewhere, a woman is dancing and obviously falling under the influence of the drug we'd seen the woman outside using. In fact, as the camera pans the club, it would appear that there are quite a number of people under the influence. Meanwhile, Catherine sits at the bar and is approached by one of Buckman's henchmen, who tells her it's time. She follows him into the back room.

Outside, the SWAT team gets into place. Back in the club's office, Catherine is talking to Buckman about the new drug, and how she needs it for her people on the street to distribute. He approaches her, friendly as can be, and then reaches down to rip out the wire she's wearing. SWAT breaks in and takes care of the situation.

Next day, Joe and Catherine are congratulated for a job well done. Joe points out that Buckman took the immunity bargaining Catherine offered, and they gathered a composite of what the supplier looked like. Outside of that, he really didn't have much to give them, except that the supplier insisted on being paid in gold coins. Detective Morelo states that the whole operation is crazy, and leaves the room. Catherine follows and asks the man what's bothering him. He tells her that everyone is so busy slapping each other on the back, that they haven't realized that they've screwed everything up. Finally he shouts that they could have nailed Buckman any time, and that the whole purpose of the operation was to get the supplier while he was still there. Then Catherine takes note of his fiance in a photograph, and compliments her. A lab technician approaches them and explains that his studies of the drug have yielded some pretty interesting information. It is organic, bacterial in nature, and glows in the dark as though it came from the darkness of caves of the depths of the ocean. This immediately strikes a chord with Catherine.

She goes to the underground to meet with Vincent, and tells him what the studies of the drug have revealed. While she's not accusing any of the Underground people of being involved, the supplier is like a mysterious shadow; someone who doesn't seem to exist apart from his drug transactions. There have been nine deaths linked to the drug, says Catherine as she hands a sample over to Vincent. She is about to leave, when he tells her that while confronting her fears is important, she must not put herself in danger. "You survived once," he says in regards to the night he found her in the park. Catherine counters, "Because I survived then, I'm doing this now. So that others are spared." Vincent cannot argue with her on this point.

The supplier makes his way through an alley carrying a large parcel. He ducks into a building, and then through an entrance to the Underground. Catherine's suspicions were correct! He moves through the tunnels. Elsewhere in the Underground, Vincent and Father are discussing the situation, with Vincent adding that the unusual thing is that the supplier insisted on gold coins in return for the drug. This affects Father, who brings up the name of a man who was banished years ago in the first test of his government. The man's name was John Pata, but he referred to himself as Paracelsus, after the alchemist who was his idol because the man was a scientist and something of a magician. "John was all of those things," says Father. "A large part of what we've created here we owe to him." Father conjectures that perhaps while seeking knowledge, Paracelsus began to yearn for power as well, and was ultimately exiled...forcefully so...so another area of the tunnels. Vincent asks him if he knows where the man is now. Father nods his head slowly.

Catherine and Morelo are in the police station at one in the morning, when he says that he's got to go meet a friend, who happens to be a "night person." She feels that he's not being completely honest with her. Finally he admits that he's got a new lead which may be a long shot, but it's worth following up. Catherine says he should bring backup, but after the disastrous (in his opinion) results in the nightclub, he'd rather do it on his own. How, she asks, does he know this isn't a set-up? He doesn't, but it's a risk worth taking. She wants to go with him, but he refuses.

Father, guided by lantern light, is moving through the tunnels and into an area flooded with bats. They fly towards him, and then are mysteriously gone. He continues until he sees Paracelsus. The man looks up, and asks how he found him. Father says they've always known where he was, and they just wanted to make sure that he wasn't thinking of returning. The man says he's quite happy where he is, and then compliments Father on the ingenious idea of communicating via the pipes. He adds that by having everyone call him Father, it gives him all the authority he needs without anyone feeling him a despot. Then he dismisses Father's dream of the Underground, adding that the two of them could have been gods. Naturally this is nothing that Father was ever interested in.

When asked why he has come, Father states that the man's activities could bring attention to the Underground. Paracelsus says they'll never catch him, and when the deaths he is causing are brought to his attention, his reaction is that this area is beyond Father's influence. And there is certainly no way they will go to the police to reveal his whereabouts, because he would reveal all there is to know about the Underground. There is only one way Father can stop him: murder!

This scene possesses terrific chemistry between the two actors, as we feel the underlying pain both are feeling. Paracelsus, exiled and denied the opportunity to be a god to the people of the underground, is jealous of Father's position. And Father regrets the original exile of the man, and feels partly responsible for his activities on the surface. If not exiled, would Paracelsus still have had an interest in the world above?

Later, Paracelsus starts to come out of the tunnels and into the basement of a building, when

Morelo steps out of the darkness, his gun levelled at the man. Morelo demands to see the contents of his bag. Paracelsus says he doesn't hear very well and explains that he's lost. Morelo again says that he wants to know what's in the bag. Paracelsus replies that it contains family crystals. Then a hidden blade in his sleeve comes down, and he stabs it viciously into Morelo's stomach. A moment later, the man drops to the ground. Paracelsus steps over the body and begins climbing the stairs.

The police, as well as Catherine and Joe, arrive on the scene of the murder. She's devastated to learn that Morelo's been killed. Catherine collapses into Joe's arms. Several hours later, she meets with Vincent and tells him that a friend was murdered. He can feel her pain, and is sorry for her. Vincent explains that she was right about the supplier coming from his world. Catherine's immediate reaction is to tell him that the man must be turned over to the authorities, but Vincent tries to explain their dilemma, that the man has sworn he would betray the secret of the Underground. It is her suggestion that the man suffer to the fullest extent of their laws. It's too late for that, Vincent says. The ultimate punishment has been enforced exile. Vincent explains that they are currently struggling for a solution, but she snaps that she can't wait. The more time that passes, the more lives are put at risk. While he can understand what she is saying, Vincent says she must live by her conscience, while they live by the laws which have allowed them to survive for so long. He retreats back into the tunnels.

This is the first time we've seen a real stand-off between Catherine and Vincent, with both wanting the same thing, but having to obtain their goals in different ways. It's a very different approach to these two characters who have always seemed very much in sync.

The council is meeting, with everyone debating what they should do. Winslow repeats Paracelsus' words: the only way to stop him is to kill him. Father wants to know if he is willing to be the man's executioner. Winslow suggests a lottery, but this, too, meets with a negative reaction from Father. Ultimately, Vincent says that they must do *something* so that two worlds are not compromised by one man's evil. Vincent will stop the man from leaving the tunnels, which will provide them with the opportunity to come up with a more "permanent" solution.

At police headquarters, one cop suggests that perhaps the supplier lives in the building where Morelo was killed, or underneath it. Catherine says that this is a crazy idea, but he adds that they know for a fact that hundreds of transients live in the steam tunnels underneath the Waldorf, and they should sweep the place. Joe thinks that it might not be a bad idea, but the Captain agrees with Catherine. The cop who asked the question and his partner can keep an eye on the place.

Paracelsus starts making his way to the surface. While he's still in the tunnels, he senses that someone is following him. He climbs out of the tunnel and into the building where Morelo had been killed. He is pursued by Vincent. They run through the basement. The man reaches a corridor, throws a handful of the sparkling drug into the air and departs. Vincent follows through a moment later, and is covered in the drug. The effect is immediate. He tries to fight it off, but is losing his struggle. He roars in fury, slams into walls and ultimately collapses. Then he starts crawling back through the tunnels until the drug takes full effect. He actually bursts through a stone wall and like an animal infected with the madness of rabies, howls furiously as his mind paints the image of a burning hell. Within that hell is the image of Catherine beckoning him on, trying to lure him into the fire.

Director Thomas J. Wright handles the drug scenes quite effectively, with a triple image overlay of the person affected that creates disorientation.

Father is reading when he hears a crashing sound. He follows it until he reaches Vincent. He can see the madness on his face, and backs away as Vincent snarls at him viciously. Father approaches him, trying to provide consolation, but is struck and sent reeling backwards. Vincent moves in for the kill, when Winslow and others run in with torches, which send Vincent fleeing further into the tunnels (suffice to say, it's quite a shocking moment to see Vincent strike Father with such viciousness, as everything we've seen of him so far belies this type of image).

Later, Catherine is meeting with Father and is told of what happened. She wants to go seek Vincent out, but Father is against the idea. Catherine argues that their tests have proven the drug wears off in three or four hours. Then again, perhaps the empathic connection between Catherine and Vincent will somehow get through the effects of the drugs. The two of them start moving through the tunnels and Catherine calls out to Vincent. They hear a low growling. As Catherine approaches Vincent, Vincent sees the image of Catherine that beckoned him into the flames earlier. He snarls viciously, and foams at the mouth, but Catherine keeps on coming. Vincent steps out of hiding and looks as though he is about to strike out at Catherine, when Vincent throws his head back trying to fight off the image. Despite the truly frightening scene before her, Catherine gets close enough to embrace Vincent lovingly. This seems to have the desired effect as he returns from the madness.

This is an interesting variation on the original **Beauty and the Beast** premise, as in that version the kiss from the beautiful princess turned the beast into a prince. In this reprise, a show of undying love and support is enough to make his mind and spirit overcome the effect of the drugs.

In his chamber later on, Vincent is feeling ashamed of what he almost did, and how he was acting. He also expresses how grateful he is to Catherine for all that she's done. Father enters the room and tells Vincent that everyone is ready to convene a Council meeting, but Vincent says the time for that has passed. Father says that it is not Vincent's responsibility to deal with Paracelsus, but Vincent disagrees. He has seen the man's demons; he has experienced the madness that the drug is bringing to both worlds. The man must be dealt with. Vincent leaves.

Vincent goes to Paracelsus' chamber, and tells the man that he must leave. The man, playing innocent, says that he's no match for Vincent, and he will do what Vincent says, but first he would like to tell Vincent the truth about himself. Paracelsus tells Vincent that Father's tale of his being found outside St. Vincent's hospital is a lie, and that Paracelsus knows the truth. He nears Vincent, releases his hidden sleeve-blade and slashes him across the chest. Vincent roars out as he backs away and into a table. A lantern is dropped, and a fire begins. Paracelsus tries to stab him again and again, but Vincent is too fast for him. Vincent lifts the man up and hurls him against a wall. Paracelsus is then surrounded by flame. He leaps over the fire, points his blade at Vincent and then realizes that his gold is melting. He runs into the fire to retrieve it, and Vincent, believing him dead, walks out of that section of tunnel.

Afterwards, Vincent is talking to Catherine, finally understanding why she takes so many risks. "There are some risks worth taking," she says. Vincent adds that there are some things worth risking everything for.

This episode effectively comments on the drug problem which faces our nation while also supplying Vincent with a worthy adversary. As we would see, Paracelsus would be back one more time during the course of the first season, and also in one of the first episodes of the second.

Episode Fifteen

"Temptation"

Written by David Peckinpah

Directed by Gus Trikonis

Catherine is in her plastic surgeon's office, who is very pleased with the way her face has healed over the past year since her attack in the park. He offers to remove one final scar near her ear, but she refuses. This surprises him, and he asks whether she'd like to put the whole thing behind her and wipe the slate clean. Catherine says that it's something she's used to, and since this has been the most wonderful year of her life, there's no reason to remove it. The doctor is nonplussed.

The DA is pleased with the progress that Joe and Catherine have made with the Taylor case, which involves an importing business as a money laundering operation for the mob. The DA wants just a little bit more information before they proceed. Joe accepts this. He and Catherine leave the office and enter into their own area.

Father and Vincent are going over Mouse's plans for a ventilation system to be utilized in the lower levels of the Underworld, which are conceptually brilliant but impossible to bring to fruition. Vincent states that he's going to visit a mythical area known as the Crystal Cavern in search of a gift for Catherine, as it has been a year since she first entered his life. Smiling, he says he can't wait to see what the next year brings, adding that at one time he rued the day the two of them met, and now is amazed at the fondness he feels for her. "You two share something quite extraordinary," Father says. "Something that touches the best in all of us."

This means a lot to Vincent, as it does for the audience. This is a *major* turning point in Father's attitude towards Catherine. We knew that it was gradually changing from episode to episode, but this is the first time he has openly admitted his feelings towards her. It's a particularly significant moment in that it demonstrates a continual growth in the characters, and shows that, like real people, they will continue to change as time goes on.

Catherine is preparing for a party being given for the Mayor of New York. There she meets up with Joe, who, like Catherine, is sheepishly without a date. Catherine goes over to meet the mayor. This is intercut with the image of Vincent making his way through unfamiliar tunnels in search of the Crystal Cavern. Back at the party, Joe meets a woman named Erica Salvan, a lawyer for another law firm, and the attraction between the two of them is immediate as they begin to dance with each other. Catherine sees them and smiles.

Vincent pauses in his journey to rest, and reads a passage which triggers a flood of memories. We are witness via a montage of clips from previous episodes. Then we're back at the party, where everyone except Joe and Erica are winding down. Next day at work, Joe tells Catherine what a wonderful night they had, and she mentions that the law firm she's working at is the one representing Taylor. Could there be a conflict of interest? He tells her not to worry.

Despite his confidence, that evening at dinner, Joe asks Erica about it, but she says she doesn't know anything about Taylor; he's not someone she has ever, or would ever, have contact with. Next day in her office, Erica is visited by her boss who asks her about Joe Maxwell, and we swiftly learn that they have to "break him down" quickly, before the trial of Taylor begins. Erica says that she's aware of the time limitation. Her boss suggests a job offer, and she replies that she'll check it out. As he leaves, we can see that this is causing her some emotional pain.

Later, Joe comes to visit Erica at the office, and is immediately taken by the luxury. In her bedroom shortly thereafter, he is holding a crystal paperweight in his hands, and jokingly says that he doesn't want to go to work. She suggests that they "call in sick," but he says he's got too much work to do. Nonetheless, he doesn't exactly jump out of bed. Erica mentions that the recruiters from her firm were looking at him, proving that he didn't have to stay stuck in the DA's office if he doesn't want to be.

Catherine sees Joe later in his office, and is a little surprised that he hasn't gotten to the Taylor deposition yet. She's thrilled that he's in love, but since he's met Erica, he seems to have lost his edge. This angers Joe, who wonders if she's accusing him of backing away from the Taylor case. She says he's acting like a moon-struck teenager who won't do his homework. Her point made, she leaves.

Vincent finally reaches the beautiful Crystal Chamber, an area where the walls themselves seem to consist primarily of crystal, each of them reflecting light.

That night, Joe is playing a little one-on-one basketball with the janitor in the office. Catherine shows up and apologizes, but he tells her not to worry about it. There's just been a lot on his mind, including, as he announces, the fact that Erica's firm is supposedly going to be making him an offer. This would be a dream come true. The DA's office is fine, but now that he's made a name for himself, he's ready to move on. Playing Devil's Advocate once again, Catherine wants to know how this potential offer will effect the Taylor investigation. He says that he's going to pull out of it, because it would be a conflict of interest. She can't accept this, because his departure would cause them to lose the momentum they've gathered on the case thus far. If the firm is really interested in him, they would wait until after the trial was over. Joe dismisses this, stating that the trial could take months, and he doesn't want to wait. Catherine laughs derisively, noting that it gives Brannigan (the other firm's leader) more time while simultaneously neutralizing Joe from the case. Ignoring this, Joe carries on about the luxury of their office, and Catherine is finding this hard to accept. Is that what he really wants? It certainly doesn't feel like him. "You're worth more than this," she states.

The next day, as Joe sits at his desk, he receives a call from Erica. They make a dinner date for nine that evening. At the restaurant, he tells her that after thinking about it carefully, he has decided they shouldn't see each other until *after* the Taylor investigation. Erica believes that he's over-reacting, but he says that even if her firm is thinking of recruiting him, it would be a conflict of interest. She turns it around, stating that what he's really trying to say is that he's afraid of a commitment, which he vehemently argues isn't true. Upset, she leaves the restaurant and he follows her out. Dropping her off at her apartment, Erica says nothing as she gets out of his car. Pulling away, Joe is suddenly followed by a police car, whose lights start flashing. Joe, law-abiding citizen that he is, pulls over. The cops get out of their car, guns drawn, and tell him to get up against the car. One of the cops checks his I.D., and says he can go. They only pulled him over because he fit the identification of someone they were after. Then the second cop comes over with a plastic bag of cocaine that he says he found under the floorboard in Joe's car. Joe can't believe what's going on as he's arrested.

The next day, Catherine is reading a newspaper and is stunned to see the article about Joe's arrest. She goes to the DA himself and complains that this is a set-up. He agrees, stating that everything goes on a back-burner until the situation is cleared up. She goes to Joe's apartment, telling him there's no way they can make the charge stick. There was no robbery and no get-away car, so there wasn't any reason for the police to pull him over. He's furious because the damage has been done in the form of the newspaper headline, and at Erica for what she's done to him. He's convinced that she's responsible.

Catherine goes to see Erica, and is quite smug with her. Erica states that she doesn't believe the charges against Joe, but Catherine won't hear any of it, stating that Erica only had one reason for getting involved in the first place: to get him to back off from the Taylor case. Catherine states that there must be some decency in her, or else Joe wouldn't have fallen in love. Could she so easily throw him away like this? Erica tells her to leave and before she does, Catherine tells the woman to search her heart. If she finds any true feelings for Joe, then Erica should phone her.

Mouse is at work in his lab, when Vincent arrives and tells him of his journey to the Crystal Cavern. Vincent pulls out a raw crystal for him, and then a second one for Catherine, which is to be worn around her neck. Vincent asks if Mouse can help refine the crystal into a true gift. Mouse says he'll put a chain through it, polish it up, and so on. This delights Vincent, who's asked what it's like to be in love. His feeling is that for everyone it must be different, but for him meeting Catherine was the beginning of a new life, and the end of his loneliness.

At home, Catherine is in the middle of sewing something for Vincent. Meanwhile, Brannigan enters Erica's office, angry that Catherine Chandler was there, and suspects her involvement. Brannigan tells Erica that this is the time for her to act tough. Her response is that there was no need to have drugs placed in Joe's car. Brannigan hopes Erica hasn't confused her loyalties. Catherine gets a phone call from Erica, who wants to talk. Erica doesn't want to leave her office because she believes someone is waiting for her. Catherine is on her way.

Catherine arrives at Erica's office. Erica immediately says that she didn't know anything about the drugs, and goes on to explain that Brannigan was seeking information to slow the Taylor investigation down. Before Erica goes on, Catherine suggests that they get out of the building to do their talking. They move to the elevator and see a shadow in the corridor. A figure steps out of the darkness and contacts the security officer in the lobby, telling him that Chandler and Erica are on their way down. The guard levels his weapon at the elevator door, but when it opens there is no one inside.

Catherine and Erica are running down flights of stairs, pursued by the man who had contacted the security guard. The guard starts running up from below. The guard reaches them and pulls his gun, but Catherine quickly dispatches him. The other man pulls his gun and is about to fire, when Vincent, like the Lone Ranger once again, leaps out of hiding and takes care of the man in his usual fashion. Vincent runs off before Erica has a chance to look at his face.

Several days later, the charges against Joe have been dropped, and everything is fine with his career. Joe thanks Catherine for all the help she provided in his troubled period. He steps into the conference room, where Erica is waiting for him. Erica is sorry for what she had done, and begs his forgiveness, hoping that when the case is over, they'll have the opportunity to get together. Joe acknowledges that the possibility does exist.

That night, Catherine is on her terrace lighting candles, when Vincent seems to blow in with the wind. He is touched that she, too, has remembered their anniversary. He gives her the crystal gift and hangs it around her neck. Catherine is moved to tears, and then gives him a rose given to her by her mother that was used as a symbol to help overcome fear. Whenever Catherine would get frightened she would look at the rose, then think of her mother and feel safe again.With the rose is a pouch that she sewed for him. "Until you came into my life," Catherine says, "I'd forgotten what it was like to know that there was someone thinking of me." This she hangs around his neck in the same fashion.

Again, the almost kiss....(sigh)

Although this episode was an enjoyable one, it's not as effective as some of the others.

Catherine and Vincent merely serve as sidemen to the story. Certainly its admirable of the producers to give the other members of the cast the opportunity to strut their stuff, but we're "paying" to see the leads. As was the situation in "Masques," where the storyline interweaved the Vincent/Catherine romance with political statements, the episode doesn't truly come alive until Catherine and Vincent are together again, expressing their love for each other. Somehow sequences like that never seem to get boring, no matter how many times they're done.

Episode Sixteen

"Promises of Someday"

Written by George R.R. Martin

Directed by Thomas J. Wright

A man named Sanders arrives in New York from Australia, goes through customs and into a men's room, where he shaves off his beard and changes his clothes. We see a series of scars running across his left cheek.

When Catherine walks into Joe's office, she's introduced to Jeff Radler, the DA's newest employee in the trial division. We recognize him as the man called Sanders in the airport. She's a bit put off by the announcement that she will be working with this newcomer on the Arringer file, which is due to be finished in several days. Later, when Jeff is alone in his office, he goes through his attache case which is filled with money. Catherine arrives a moment later and he closes it. Jeff leaves and Catherine is about to follow several hours later, when Joe corners her and asks that she drop something off at Jeff's hotel.

Just as Catherine arrives at the building, she catches sight of Jeff, who is walking into the park. He approaches a closed down carousel, and has a memory flash to an earlier time when it was still operating. We hear the laughter of children, and then the memory ends. He climbs the fence blocking it off, and seems to be allowing the memories to wash over him. Then he's back over the fence and making his way through the park until he finds the entrance to the storm tunnel we've seen many times in the past. He enters it, and is followed, secretly, by Catherine. Moving to the metal gate that blocks further passage, he rubs away some dirt on the stone wall and finds initials which were carved there years earlier. Another flashback, and we see Jeff and a very young Vincent in the midst of carving their initials. He proceeds down another tunnel, thus allowing Catherine to take a look at the initials.

The next day Catherine is talking business with Jeff, but she doesn't bring up the previous night. That afternoon, she goes back to the tunnels where she meets Vincent and tells him of Jeff Radler, but the name doesn't mean anything to him. She voices her suspicion that the man seems to know about the Underworld, and mentions the carved names she found. Catherine does her best to describe the man, right down to the scars on his left cheek. The description strikes a chord with Vincent, but he says the time isn't right to discuss it.

Going back to his chamber, Vincent looks over some mementos which were obviously very important to him as a youth, including a toy carousel. Back at the DA's office, Jeff is obviously distraught about something. Catherine enters his office, but he excuses himself, stating that he has to see someone regarding an apartment. He leaves, and she catches sight of a crumpled piece of paper, which is then unfolded, and whatever is on it disturbs her. Catherine brings the paper to Joe, who dismisses it as the result of nervousness. Apparently there is something wrong with his notes regarding the case they're working on.

Once again back at his hotel (it's truly annoying that this story keeps jumping back and forth between day and night and various locations. It brings with it the sense of an episodic nature),

Jeff is packing a bag and he returns to the park. In another flashback, a police officer on horseback confronts the Underground children who are on the ride. When he calls out to them, they panic and run for cover. Flashback over, he starts moving into the tunnels again. With a large metal cutter, he snaps the lock on the gate, and is about to proceed. Then the metal door swings open and Vincent is standing there, referring to him as Devin, which no one has done for twenty years. The two embrace warmly. Finally Vincent says they had spent months searching for him when he disappeared twenty years earlier, and that Father had thought him lost in the maze. Devin explains that he just had to get out of the Underground. Changing the subject, he wants to know how Vincent knew he was going to be there. He is told that Catherine Chandler had followed him the night before and told Vincent of it. This is a shocking announcement to Devin, who remarks on the small world they live in. Then he asks how Father (who he refers to as the old man) is. Vincent offers to take Devin to him, but Devin doesn't believe that would be a very good idea, as the two of them never really got along.

Devin explains that he's been all over the world, and yet recently he's been having dreams of the tunnels. Vincent remarks that such dreams should not be disregarded, when this "hole in the ground is home." He brings Devin to Father, who is shocked beyond words, but also seems delighted. Unfortunately the delight turns to recrimination, as Father scolds the man for never getting word to them that he was still alive. Father reminds Devin of the pain that he caused. This is all very upsetting to Devin, who apologizes for everything, and states that he would like to start over again. Father says that would be a wonderful idea. Devin explains that he is now a lawyer, and before that he was a hunter in Kenya and a monk in Tibet. "I've been just about everything by now," he says, almost sadly.

Father lashes into him again when he learns that Devin has been moving from one occupation in life to another without any training of any sort, including as a doctor who delivered a baby via c-section. Does he realize the peril he put that woman through? Devin flashes back to an earlier era, when Father was yelling at him for his lack of responsibility, and the fact that he, Vincent and others were nearly caught on the surface by a police officer because they wanted to have some fun. What would have happened had Vincent been caught? What would have become of him? Unlike in the past, Devin fights back, stating that Father, despite all his brilliant medical knowledge, couldn't save his mother during childbirth. Devin picks up his bag and is gone.

Granted there is more to this story still to unfold, but at this point Father really isn't very likable. Undoubtedly he had good reason to yell at Devin as a child, but he has reverted back to that frame of mind some twenty years later, thus alienating the man and causing himself great pain as well. In this sequence, he is uncharacteristically lacking in sympathy.

Devin moves into a vast "wind-tunnel" area, where he flashes back to a fight he was having as a child with Vincent, which quickly turned into a fistfight. He punched Vincent in the face, resulting in a bloody nose, and the usual peaceful Vincent struck back, slashing the other boy's left cheek. The flashback ends as the adult Vincent places a hand on Devin's shoulder. As Devin picks up his bag to leave again, he states that perhaps because Father wasn't able to save his mother, the man sees that failure every time he looks into Devin's face. Vincent asks if he'll be back, but Devin's response is that he may return in another twenty years or so, adding that the baby he delivered, as well as its mother, are both doing fine. And then, Devin is gone.

Vincent goes to see Catherine, describing how lost Devin seems. While Catherine can sympathize, she points out that his masquerade may put a child molester back on the streets, and she can't allow that to happen. Vincent tries to ignore this, explaining that Devin was the only one among his friends who dreamed dreams that included him. Theirs was a very close and meaningful relationship, which is why her decision to expose him will pain Vincent. Devin will be gone again. She apologizes with all her heart, truly believing that there is no other alternative.

Next day, Devin is at work when Catherine enters his office and tells him that she won't go to the police, but she wants him off the Arringer case. He tells her not to worry about it, adding that he'll be out of the DA's office by night. Catherine asks him why he has moved from one occupation to another, and his reply is a simple one: as a child he never knew what he wanted to be as a grown-up.

The character of Devin, incidentally, seems to be borrowed from an episode of **M*A*S*H**, in which a visiting surgeon turns out to be a fraud, albeit a brilliant one. The simple truth of the matter is that he's a genius, and excels at just about everything he tries his hand at. It was his opinion that he didn't have to spend half his life in school, when he would know how to do *anything* just by doing some basic research. Devin really seems to be an extrapolation of that character.

Vincent and Father are discussing the situation with Devin, and Vincent is shocked to hear Father say that Devin's departure is a good thing, because he will only bring them pain. Vincent chastises Father for being so hard on Devin the previous night, but Father's reaction is to say he has always been hard on the boy for his own good; to help him grow up into a responsible adult. Father talks of the past (the flashback we've already been witness to), stating that Devin's escapades endangered everyone...particularly Vincent. Vincent will not hear this, stating categorically that Father was harder on Devin than on anyone else. Then the bombshell is dropped by Father: the year after he lost everything in his life (including Margaret), when he nearly froze to death that winter, a woman named Grace told him of the tunnels, and showed him the way down. Underground, he slowly began to live again, and he and Grace fell in love. The result of their love was Devin, who was born as Grace lost her life. Vincent is stunned to hear that Devin is Father's son.

That night, Catherine shows up at Devin's door and is allowed to enter. She tells him that he shouldn't leave New York, because of the pain it will bring to Vincent. This seems to infuriate him, as he's tired of people always being concerned about Vincent. She brings up the night at the carousel, and he brings her down to the park. They reach the ride, with Devin explaining that when he was a boy, Father had forbidden him to have a knife. He saved the money he could find and bought one anyway, and someone told Father. He had assumed it was Vincent, and after the fight (which we had seen via flashback) between them, he discovered that a boy named Mitch had told, but by then the damage was done. Another flashback shows the young Devin breaking into the ride area with other children, including Vincent and getting on the horses. But then a cop showed up and began pursuing them. The cop had grabbed Devin, but let him go when Vincent leaped out of hiding, growling. The cop levelled his gun at the youth, but Devin threw a rock which caught the man in the head, and sent him reeling backwards into the lake. The two of them ran off to safety. And Father, naturally, took the whole incident out on him, asking if he wanted Vincent to get caught because of the fight they had. "Yes," screamed the young Devin. "He's a freak, and I hate him."

Flashback over, Devin says that he didn't really mean it. There were times when he felt that way...but not that time. Catherine wants to know why he never told Father the truth. Perhaps pride, or...his sentence is interrupted by Father and Vincent, who approach, with the former suggesting that perhaps the biggest problem between them was that they had never learned to talk to each other. Father says that Devin deserves to know the truth, and calls him son. This seems to melt Devin's defenses, and he senses the truth in the man's words. Father starts to tell the tale of his past, his life before the Underground and the relationship he had with Devin's mother.

Catherine, meanwhile, shows Vincent Devin's brief on the Attinger case, and is a bit amazed to see that, despite some rough areas, it should be strong enough to keep the man in prison for a long time. She asks if he thinks Devin will stay, but Vincent responds in the negative. Devin has always dreamed of travelling to different places, but now...at the very least...he has somewhere to come home to. The episode ends with a dissolve to Devin going to an airport and buying a ticket to Alaska. When asked his name, he replies, "Wells. Devin Wells." This, of course, was Father's real family name.

While this is a solid episode, its does show a disquieting repetition of elements. For starters, there is much too much use of flashback, which is a valid storytelling tool once or twice but becomes a bit much when used too often. Then there's also the idea of someone returning to the tunnels who has been gone for a number of years, which was the same basic plot as the sixth episode, "The Beast Within." Undoubtedly the producers were aware of this as well, as Devin mentions another childhood friend named Mitch, who was something of a troublemaker. Referring back to the episode cited above, we see that the returnee to the tunnels was Mitch as well. Thus the idea is that they've tried to create a three-way friendship that went off in different directions. Unfortunately it seems a thin veil designed to cover similar plotlines. Still, the cast does a very nice job with the material, and the further development of Father's background is wonderful.

Episode Seventeen

"Down to a Sunless Sea"

Written by Don Balluck

Directed by Christopher Leitch

Vincent stirs restlessly in his bed, having visions of running through what appears to be a forest. Then, he's awake.

At the DA's office, Catherine is talking to the victim of wife abuse, telling her that she must remember what her husband did to her—even *after* the bruises have healed. The woman doesn't like the idea of pressing charges against the man she married, feeling that she couldn't stand to see him locked up. She tries to convince Catherine and Joe, as well as herself, that her husband's promise that this will never happen again is true. Naturally no one buys it. When she leaves, we can see how frustrated Catherine and Joe are. At that moment, Catherine gets a call from a friend of hers named Jenny, who explains that she had just gotten a phone call from a man named Stephen Bass, to whom she gave Catherine's phone number. The name obviously means something to Catherine.

That evening, Catherine is listening to her answering machine, and finds a message from Stephen Bass, who says that he wants to speak to her about something very important. He leaves his number and expresses his hope that she will call him back.

Flashback time once again, where we see the final moments of the relationship Catherine had once had with Bass. Apparently he's too possessive for her taste (or was) and wouldn't allow her to be her own person. Flashback ended, we dissolve to the Underground, where Vincent is reading a bedtime story to some of the children. While he reads, he flashes back to his dream in which he's running through the woods, but he manages to continue reading. Back at Catherine's apartment, Stephen (who she has obviously called) arrives, and after an awkward moment or so, he enters.

In the ensuing conversation, we've learned that it's been five years since they last saw each other, but he wants to know if they can nonetheless stop moving around each other as though they were strangers. After a moment of silence, Catherine notes, "We are strangers," which doesn't sit very well with him. They continue doing their best to talk, and he comes out with the key question: is there someone she's romantically involved with? When she replies in the affirmative, he says that he's happy for her and that things haven't been that great for him. Catherine says that she heard about his parents' death, and he comes out with the fact that he was the drunk behind the wheel that ultimately got them killed. As a result, he served six months in jail, and it's taken him the past five years to get his life back together. He adds that he has a terminal brain tumor. Catherine's heart goes out to him. She is further shocked to hear that he's only got six months left to live, which is why he's come. She's the closest friend he's got, and he'd appreciate it if she could see him once in a while—as friends, with no commitments. Yet another flashback (and this is truly getting to be an annoying story device on this show), with the two of them in the park, looking extremely happy and in love.

The next day, Bass goes to a jewelry store where he spends three thousand dollars on a special gift, although we don't know what it is. Unable to get a cab, he starts walking (one would assume) home. His journey is rudely interrupted when two punks slam him against a wall and demand his money. He suddenly fights back with a sudden viciousness that would make Vincent or Charles Bronson proud. When the two punks are out cold, he starts gathering up the contents of his spilled attache case: numerous photographs of Catherine!

In the tunnels, Catherine is telling Vincent about Bass' visit. She still feels an obligation towards him, perhaps because of the man's illness, or else because of the intimacy they once had with each other. Vincent flashes back to the run through a forest, and then he's "back." She comments on the fear she saw in his face. He asks if she's afraid of Bass, but she doesn't think that's the fitting word. Maybe curious as to the way her life might have turned out had they stayed together, coupled with the guilt she feels for hurting him. Vincent doesn't know what to say to her.

Later, Bass is being shown a very large house in the suburbs (although exactly where isn't clear) by a real estate agent. He looks around, and decides to take it.

Back Underground, Vincent is trying to describe the image he keeps seeing whenever he thinks of Catherine to Father. He says that he remembers the last time that a man entered Catherine's life and how Vincent reacted. Vincent counters that this is different. There is something intangible in his mind; a feeling of threat. "A threat to her, or to you?" Father asks.

Catherine and Bass are laughing in her apartment, reflecting on the past and seemingly getting very close with each other again, although he does give some hints of the pain he feels over their having broken up. He catches sight of the scars on Catherine's cheek, feeling that they're a "roadmap to a person's past." Flashback to the two of them breaking up, and we can see that the final argument was particularly volatile. Snapping out of it, he tells her that he had better go, and asks her to an opera the next night. She says she'd love to go with him.

Bass arrives at an establishment where he had ordered an antique stove, but it hasn't arrived. The salesman brings him over to one that has arrived for him, but is chagrined to learn that it's the wrong color. Bass wanted a red stove, not a black one. He starts shouting at the man, telling him that he absolutely needs the stove the next day because *everything* depends on it. His eyes flaring madly, he turns around and leaves.

Joe corners Catherine at work and tells her that Marcy O'Neil (the abused wife from the opening) is in jail, because she stabbed her husband and there's a fifty/fifty percent that he'll live. She proceeds to "the tombs" and tries talking to her. She is distraught, not knowing what to do. Marcy wants to know if she's going to go to prison, and Catherine tells her that it may depend on whether or not her husband lives. The woman adds that he was hitting her for absolutely no reason, and she just reached for the knife. From the look on her face, we can see that Catherine's heart is breaking for this woman.

Going to an exterior pay phone, Catherine calls Bass, who says he has to cancel out of their date because he's not feeling very well. She tells him that when she gets the opportunity, she'll stop by his hotel. From there she goes down to the tunnels, where Vincent tries to describe the image he has been seeing. Catherine really starts snapping at him, angry that he's saddling her with his vision of fear and yet unable to tell her what it represents. How is she supposed to go up to the surface and get on with her life? She's supposed to see Stephen that night, and Vincent recommends she not go. Catherine feels that she has to, because he's dying and she's all he has. Angry, she leaves.

One question really must be asked: when will Catherine learn? We know that Vincent is above jealousy, that his heart is filled with more generosity than anyone's, and yet she will not heed his words about the danger he senses.

That night, in Bass' hotel room, he tells her that the problem is that he forgot to take his medicine earlier, but now he's beginning to feel better. Catherine tries to describe her day, and the anguish of all the people who need help, and her inability to help all of them. Bass can identify, talking about a trip to India where he saw the poverty, and realized that hunger means different things to different people. Then she says she's going to have to be going because there are two hours worth of paperwork awaiting her. He tells her that she needs a change of scenery, and tells her of a house that he's thinking of buying in New Rochelle. Will she go up on Saturday with him to look at it? She pleads that there's much too much work to be done, but he manages to convince her to slip away for a couple of hours. They kiss good-bye, and Catherine leaves. As Bass closes the door, he experiences another flashback to the two of them in the park—the same flashback we had seen earlier. But as the conversation within that flashback continues, we hear them joking about the future, with Bass noting that they should get a country house, and Catherine adding that a red antique stove would be nice. Now we *know* things aren't right with this guy, particularly when the flashback ends and we take a look in his eyes.

That Saturday, Bass drives Catherine up to his new house, and it truly fills the description of their conversation several years earlier. He leads her inside, emphasizing that there is complete privacy, with woods behind them and the feeling that there is no one around for hundreds of miles. She is really taken by the place, and then she walks into the living room and he shows her the red stove. He asks if it is what she had in mind when they talked about it? Catherine honestly doesn't remember what he's talking about. He leads her into a bedroom, with photos of her in frames and a closet full of clothing. He says that she won't have to go back to pack a thing, which is another stunner for her. Frightened, she asks that he take her home. "But, Cathy," he replies with full sincerity, "you are home!"

This scene is designed to create impact. This guy has obviously blown a gasket, and we can feel the fear that is etched on Catherine's face. She starts to walk out of the house, but he quickly catches up just as she finds the front door locked. "You're not being reasonable," he says, truly sounding like Norman Bates.

In the tunnels, Vincent feels what's happening to her. Back at the house she tries to climb out a window, but he grabs her, proclaiming his love. When she resists, he knocks her over the head with an object, and she slips into unconsciousness. Vincent screams out in the tunnel, and begins running. When she awakens, Catherine is tied to a chair at the dining room table. Stephen Bass simply does not see any problem. We intercut with the image of Vincent riding on top of a subway car, and then cut back to the house, where Bass is extremely disappointed at Catherine's reaction to his trying to give her everything she's ever wanted. She points out that all this is what she described in the past, but he doesn't want to hear that. Moving closer, he states that no one could ever love her the way that he does, and he forces a kiss on her. We cut back to Vincent, who's riding the top of a train *outside* the safety of the tunnels. In the house, Stephen is still trying to force the issue, but Catherine manages to get free and smashes him across the face, sending him reeling to the floor. She bolts away and actually leaps through the window to the ground below.

Vincent, living out the vision he has been experiencing throughout the episode, is now running through the woods, breathing heavily. Meanwhile, Catherine has gotten to her feet and is running with all her might. Bass calls out her name and starts off in pursuit. Vincent moves through the woods. Catherine runs for her life. Bass follows, closing in rapidly, and then tackles her to the ground and wraps his hands around her neck, shouting that he never wanted it to be this way. He is quite literally choking the life out of her. "Why can't it be like it was before?" he demands.

As though in answer, Vincent is there, slamming him against the ground and then against a tree, slashing and pummeling him. Catherine pulls Vincent away, stating that it's over. Vincent expels a breath of air, which, incidentally, he has done every time he has come down from one of his violent episodes, and almost gives the impression of having just gone through an orgasmic experience. Perhaps his explosions of violence against those who prey on the innocent allow a cathartic release. Whatever the case may be, he picks up the body of Bass and starts carrying it back to the house.

Later, at Catherine's home, she tells Vincent that "they" wouldn't let her see Bass, and she essentially apologizes for misjudging Vincent's fear that danger was awaiting her. When she asks how he knew of the danger, his response is that perhaps it is because deep within her *she* must have known.

"Down to a Sunless Sea" works wonderfully as a study of obsession, and comes across as a particularly *true* story in terms of dramatic intent. Each of us is obsessed with *something*, and it really is a question of degree. In the case of Stephen Bass, his relationship with Catherine proved to be something he couldn't let go of, despite the fact that five years had passed since they broke up. Like most intense obsessions, this was a truly frightening one, leading you to believe that he would have stopped at nothing to recreate the relationship that once was, but could never be again. Interesting too, but not really explored, is that this episode represented the first time that Vincent had strayed from the confines of the city and was in a relatively dangerous environment.

Episode Eighteen

"Fever"

Written by Mark and Michael Cussutt

Directed by Thomas J. Wright

In the Underground, Mouse is chipping through a wall, when he finds a hidden chamber and something special within, although we don't know what it is. Elsewhere, one of the teenagers approaches Colin, who has just finished carving a chess piece that looks like Vincent, which will be a part of a set he is making for Father for the mid-winter feast. He tells her that it's a surprise, and asks that she keep it a secret.

Catherine arrives in the Underground, bearing things that she has brought from her apartment. Vincent looks through the items and suggests that in the future she remove the price tags from the "knick-knacks" she brings from home. They share a laugh over this, although she tries to ignore the comment. She gives Father a sweater, and hands Mouse a present just as he runs in: tools, which he finds a very touching and exciting gesture. Having given out the gifts, Catherine says that she's got to go, and Vincent offers to escort her out. When they're gone, Father speaks of erosion on the upper levels, and that there is a leak from one of the major sewer pipes. Colin fears that the city's workers may come looking for the problem, and suggests they survey the situation and do something about it themselves, if possible. Mouse suddenly runs off, much to Winslow's chagrin, but nobody puts up too much of a fight.

As they're moving towards the tunnel exit, Vincent notes that Catherine's gifts have brought much joy to the people of the Underworld. She only wishes she could do more, but he points out that her generosity and friendship are the ultimate gifts. Mouse suddenly catches up to them, and hands a gift to Catherine, which is wrapped in a pouch. He asks her to wait to open it at home. With that, the boy is gone.

Back at home, Catherine phones her girlfriend Jenny, and tells her that she's running a little late, but that she'll meet her at the bookstore. She opens Mouse's gift, and finds that it is a very rare looking and beautiful necklace, which she puts on for her evening out.

Mouse brings Colin and Winslow to his chamber, looking for something, when Colin takes note of a gold plate that Mouse says he found. Winslow nears Colin and they see all kinds of gold and silver objects. Winslow asks that he show them where he found the material, and his response is "It's only gold." They convince him to show them the location, provided that they're willing to keep it a secret. The three of them go to the cavern that Mouse had discovered at the outset of the episode, and are astounded to find a cutlass within what they discover to be an ancient ship that must have been trapped for centuries. Then they find a treasure chest filled with gold, rubies, antique jewelry, and the like.

Colin and Winslow are thrilled to find the gold, which isn't very surprising when you consider that both men are from the surface. Mouse, on the other hand, doesn't think that highly of gold, having most likely spent the majority of his life Underground. This is a very interesting glimpse of the comparative mores from above and below.

As Mouse climbs out of the ship, Colin calls out that he shouldn't tell anyone about this discovery. Winslow tells him not to worry about it, as the boy probably won't tell anyone "except his damn raccoon." Colin figures the boy doesn't even realize what he's found, and when he starts staring intently at the booty, Winslow comments that the boy may be the smart one at that.

Catherine arrives at the book signing, where she meets her friend Jenny, the publicist behind the visiting publisher. As Jenny goes over to speak to the author, a man named Jonathan Thorpe who introduces himself as "without me this book could never have been written." He kisses her hand, staring at her necklace, and commenting on how beautiful it is. The author is about to say hello to Catherine, when Jonathan pulls him away.

Colin is a bit annoyed that Mouse has brought a group of children to the area so that they can help bring the gold back home. Winslow points out that it doesn't matter, as it belongs to all of them anyway.

At work the next day, Catherine gets a call from Jonathan Thorpe, who wants to speak to her over lunch and she accepts —for a woman so in love with Vincent, Catherine certainly goes out with a lot of different men. During their lunch, he mentions that he's interested in the necklace she's wearing and would like to buy it. She's not interested in selling it because it was a gift. He points out that it was probably stolen, but Catherine isn't interested in what he has to say. She leaves the restaurant.

Vincent comes to see Father, telling him that work at the site of the sewer leak is not progressing for the simple reason that no one is there. Their conversation is interrupted by a tapping on pipes which Vincent recognizes as coming from Catherine. When they're together, she tells him that the gift from Mouse is solid gold and is dated to the 17th Century. Vincent cannot believe that Mouse stole it, for the boy only takes things he actually needs, such as machine parts. Cutting to the children looking through the gold, we can see arguments already starting between them. Colin and Winslow really get into a screaming match, with Colin in particular screaming about his share of the gold. Vincent appears and stops the fight by shouting at them, which is enough to make them grow silent. He calls a Council meeting, where they will discuss the gold like friends. Before leaving with the rest, Colin puts some of the gold in his pockets.

At work, Catherine asks one of her assistants for a back-up check on Jonathan Thorpe. In the Underground, the Council meeting is in progress, with Father finding the discovery quite amazing. He assumes that after the ship sunk, the land changed over the centuries and it was covered over by shifting earth. He adds that the community must decide what to do with the gold. One woman says that it can help them in terms of food, toys for the children, machinery parts, and provide a proper thank you for some of the helpers on the surface who have aided them for so many years. These are all noble enough uses for the gold, but Colin's expression betrays the fact that it doesn't exactly fit in with his plans. Vincent points out that there is a danger in trying to use the gold to buy things; it could conceivably expose their world. Father's opinion is that it is not just gold, but also a piece of history. "These things have to be studied," he says. Winslow disagrees, asking him to repeat those words the next time they run out of penicillin. Colin steps forward, explaining that Winslow and Mouse can do what they want with their shares, but a third of it is his. These words stun everyone, particularly Vincent, who believed the man to have a generous soul. Colin feels that this is a dream come true, and ignores Vincent's response that some dreams can become nightmares. Colin talks about his life on the surface and how he had always dreamed of having nice things like other people, and this seems to be the answer he had been looking for. Father points out that that may have been true in the above world, but he has never wanted for anything since he came to the Underworld. More bickering, and Father manages to stop them. If they can't deal with it, then they should bury it. Even more arguing ensues, all of it causing Vincent great pain.

Catherine is told that Thorpe is wanted in India, Egypt and half of South American for smuggling and robbery of ancient artifacts. Back Underground, Vincent tries to console Father, who is distraught at the examples of selfishness he has witnessed. Vincent is confident that everyone will eventually come to their senses. He adds that Colin is above. A girl named Jamie had informed him that Colin had taken some gold before he vanished.

On the surface, Colin has gone to a jewelry exchange, and is trying to sell the gold he had stolen. The man offers him two thousand dollars, but when Colin refuses, he ups the offer to ten thousand, which Colin accepts, adding that he has more of the material if he wants it. The man says he can't move too much of it, but an "acquaintance" of his would probably be interested. The man hands Colin an envelope containing the ten thousand dollars and states that he has arranged a meeting for that evening at 8:30.

Colin goes back Underground, steals a sharp tool from Mouse's workbench and departs. Catherine, meanwhile, is meeting again with Vincent, and is told that Father's heart is breaking as their world is falling apart because of the gold. She adds that things are worse, as she details Thorpe's interest in her necklace. Meanwhile, Colin arrives at the area where the gold is and starts scooping up his share of the booty. Mouse is furious, telling the man it isn't worth it. He shows the boy the cash he received, but in Mouse's innocent eyes it's only paper, and not nearly as pretty as the things Colin had taken. Mouse tries to stop the man, but Colin pulls the tool out of his pocket and actually stabs Mouse, who collapses to the ground in stunned surprise. Colin hardly slows down a bit, as he departs, stepping over Mouse's fallen body.

Actually, seeing such an act of violence in the Underworld is very disturbing . Up to this point, it has been painted as a lyrical and magical place; the only violence we've witnessed has been when Vincent defended against invaders. Outside of that, everything of an unpleasant nature has taken place on the surface. This makes Colin's stabbing of Mouse very powerful.

Catherine and Vincent find Mouse, who manages to tell them that Colin did this to him, and that Colin has taken more of the gold to trade for paper. Meanwhile, Colin makes his way to the surface, torn by what he's done, but continuing nonetheless. He goes to the jewelry exchange for his meeting, where Thorpe is waiting for him. Colin tells the man that he wants fifty thousand dollars for everything. Thorpe, convinced that there's more gold, pulls a gun, states that he never pays, and tells Colin that he's going to lead him to the rest of the gold.

Catherine and Vincent meet with some of the others, and Winslow threatens to kill Colin for what he's done to Mouse. Father steps out of the other chamber, stating that Mouse has lost a great deal of blood, but he believes the boy will be alright. Suddenly there is a tapping on pipes: Colin is back, accompanied by a man with a gun. Vincent is up and on his feet again.

Colin and Thorpe near an area known as the abyss (which we had seen earlier in episode number two, "Terrible Savior"). At that moment Colin attacks the other man, but Thorpe turns out to be the superior fighter. Vincent is suddenly there, slamming Thorpe down the stairs. Thorpe raises his gun and is about to fire, when Colin throws his unidentifiable pointed tool, which imbeds itself in Thorpe's neck. Thorpe stumbles backwards and plunges into the abyss.

Catherine removes her necklace and puts it into the trunk of gold. The community is about to get rid of everything, believing that it has nearly cost them everything. Mouse and Colin make up and the two are about to throw the chest into the abyss when Vincent explains that such an action would be tantamount to admitting defeat. There may be no place for this gold in their world, but it would be very helpful to the homeless and the hungry above. They should be thought of as each of them are a part of the city, whether living below or above on the surface. As a result of his words, the gold is brought to the surface and deposited at the doorstep of the St. Regis' Home for the Homeless.

Catherine wonders what the nuns in that place must have thought on finding the gold. "That it was a miracle," is Vincent's response.

A simplistic theme handled very nicely. It is a bit hard to believe that everyone would accept Colin back so easily after what he had done to Mouse. Incidentally, the original ending of the story had the gold plunging into the abyss, but story editor Howard Gordon, among others, strongly believed that putting it to good use rather than destroying it was the only way to cap off the story properly. Certainly a good decision.

Episode Nineteen

"Everything Is Everything"

Written by Virginia Aldridge

Directed by Victor Lobl

Catherine is in the midst of backing up her car, when she hears a child crying out in pain.

Getting out of the vehicle, she runs behind it and finds a young boy (Tony) grasping his leg, and shouting. Suddenly filled with panic, Catherine says that she'll bring him to the hospital, but he refuses to go with her. Then offering to take him to his family, Tony responds that he has no family, asks her for money and promises that he'll go to see a doctor. At that moment, the boy grabs the wallet from her pocketbook and runs off. Catherine is stunned by this robbery, and the con job she has just become a victim of.

In the Underground, Vincent is listening to a group of youngsters who are studying Shakespeare, and clearly not enjoying it. He encourages them to actually *feel* the words as opposed to just reading them. Father enters the chamber, reinforcing what Vincent has just said, and the two of them read, and in so doing breathe life into, **Romeo and Juliet**, gradually enthralling the children who applaud enthusiastically upon their conclusion. Needless to say, there is no other network show on the air today that could get away with a Shakespearean performance, and pull it off so effectively.

Furious, Catherine goes to her office and tells Joe that she has to cancel all of her credit cards before Tony charges her "into bankruptcy." She also states her determination to catch the boy.

Elsewhere, Tony has gone to a auto body shop, where he is in the midst of an argument with a man named Vick Ramos, who is refusing the boy permission to see his grandfather. "We're sorry your folks got killed," says Vick, "but it don't change nothing! You're dead...marimay...banished!" Tony accuses the man of framing his father, which in turn resulted in his "banishment," but he ignores him. As Tony runs off, shouting something about having proof of what he claims, another man, named Joe, approaches and asks Vick what will happen if somebody believes the boy. "He's dead," is Vick's simple response. Meanwhile, Milo Ramos, Tony's grandfather, asks his wife Eva what all the shouting was about, but she dismisses it as nothing more than the rantings of a boy.

That night, there is a knock upon Catherine's door, and she is surprised to find Tony standing at its threshold. He hands her the wallet, claiming that he had found it on the street. He tries to apologize for what he did, but she obviously finds it difficult to trust him. He emphasizes that he needs her help. He's an orphan, and his grandfather won't see him. Again, Catherine is finding all of this hard to swallow. Finally, Tony admits that he is a gypsy and essentially summarizes the plotline for the episode by explaining, "My grandfather's King of the Gypsies...My father would have been the next king, but my uncle set him up, framed him at the...gypsy trial, and they banished us all. My uncle's gonna pay for what he did. I've got proof."

Catherine tries to find out what kind of proof he's talking about, but Tony refuses to answer, merely pleading that she allow him to spend the night there because he has nowhere else to go. Being the softie that she is, Catherine ultimately agrees to let him spend the night, provided that he take a bath and that in the morning he give her the whole story behind what he's talking about. Tony agrees to these conditions. Later, while Catherine is sleeping, the boy sneaks into her room and heads for the jewelry box, which he opens. Music begins to play, Catherine awakens and he runs out with whatever jewelry he can gather up in his hands. She tries to grab him, and is only successful in pulling a gold chain from around his neck, with the boy himself disappearing down the corridor. Frustrated, Catherine looks down at the chain, and the gold medallion attached to it, which is marked by what appears to be a family crest.

In the tunnels the next day, Catherine tells Vincent about what had happened, explaining that while she is angry at Tony, she can't help but feel concerned about the tale the boy told him. She actually believes his claim that he is considered "dead" by his family. Studying the medallion she hands him, Vincent explains that the gypsy world is a secret one, but there is a gypsy helper above who may be able to help her.

Later, Catherine goes to a luggage shop, where she meets Maria, the helper that Vincent had spoken of. The pair go to the rear of the shop, where Catherine asks whether or not it would be possible for a new gypsy trial...the kris...to be conducted so that Tony could plead his case. Maria responds that this would be quite impossible, but she nonetheless gives her Milo's address, although Vick will undoubtedly not allow her to see the old man. Catherine gives Maria her card, asks her to call should she hear from Tony, and departs the shop. From there she goes to the auto body shop we had seen earlier, spots Vick and explains that she's having car problems. Popping the hood, he takes a look and indicates that the problem is serious indeed. Acting frustrated, she asks to use the phone, and is told that there's a payphone inside the building. Entering, she spots a stairway leading to the apartments above, and inconspicuously makes her way up them. As she reaches the top of the stairs, Eva startles her by stepping out of her apartment. Catherine quickly explains that she has come to speak to the woman about Tony, but Eva starts to close the door, stating that she does not have a grandson. Before the door is closed, Catherine manages to get out that Tony has evidence which will prove his father's innocence. Eva's only response is to ask her to tell the boy that she loves him. At that exact moment, Vick begins calling up to her.

Explaining that she thought the phone was upstairs, Catherine is told that her car is a "time bomb" that's ready to go off. It is Vick's opinion that she should leave the car with him for a week, but she says that she'll take her chances and departs. Going back to her apartment, she is surprised to find Tony waiting within. Tony wants his medallion, but Catherine asks where her jewelry is. After being told that the boy hocked it, she responds that she hocked his medallion. He senses that she's lying, and goes on to explain that the medallion is all he has left of his grandfather, and without it he has nothing. Finally, she brings the medallion to him, and he hands back the jewelry he had stolen. A truce, and the beginning of a friendship, is struck. After preparing for bed, Catherine asks him if he'd like to read something from her library before he goes to sleep, and eventually learns that the boy can't read. She decides, then, to read the boy to sleep.

The images dissolves to the terrace, where Catherine is in the midst of reading to Vincent, while Tony is asleep in the apartment. She explains that the first time Vincent read to her helped Catherine to find strength and comfort, and it was something that she wanted to share with the boy. She also truly feels for his plight, and wishes that there was some way to reach his grandfather. Vincent points out that the man must somehow be convinced.

That night, Milo is awakened from sleep by the presence of Vincent in his bedroom. The man reacts in fear, but Vincent tries to calm him, explaining that he means no harm and that he has come to speak of Tony. Gathering his nerve, Milo quickly explains that he no longer has a grandson, as a result of the kris. Surely, Vincent reasons, there must be room in his heart for compassion and the desire in him to give Tony the chance to prove his father's innocence. Milo responds that if the result of the trial is the same, then he himself will lose everything he has gained among the Gypsies.

"If Tony can change the judgement," Vincent says softly, "you will have your grandson back. Can there be a greater treasure?"

Catherine awakens the next morning to find that Tony has cooked, and burned, breakfast. She is nonetheless touched by the sentiment. He goes on to thank her for reading to him, explaining that it reminded him of similar times with his mother. When he says that being alone has the tendency to make you tough, Catherine smiles and points out that she too lost her mother at a very young age, and there are still nights when she cries over the memory. When Catherine announces that she has to get ready for work, Tony says that he will take off like he promised to. She tells him to stay, pointing out that her instinct tells her that things will work out between the boy and his grandfather.

Vincent is in his chamber, lost in thought, when Father enters, explaining that they have a problem with the Chelsea entry to the tunnels. He cuts himself off, as he studies Vincent's expression, and the two of them discuss the situation of Tony and his grandfather. Father believes that there is a chance that Vincent has had an affect on Milo. After all, he reasons, "you can be most persuasive."

At the auto shop, Eva has already informed Vick and Joe that Milo will be granting Tony a new kris. Joe is panicking, wondering what will happen if the boy can prove anything. Vick says he can't, and that Milo must be getting senile. Going up to the old man's bedroom, Vick gets into a heated argument with him, saying that it's ridiculous for Tony to be granted a new kris. Eva asks Vick why he is so afraid of the new kris, but the man has no answer.

In Catherine's apartment, Tony tries to call Eva, but whoever he's speaking to refuses to connect him. Annoyed, he hangs up the phone and leaves the premises. He goes to the auto shop, and starts throwing pebbles at the upstairs window, doing his best to draw Eva's attention. Suddenly Vick is behind him, stating that he should have "stayed dead." He hauls the boy away, and starts searching him for the letter of proof that Tony had said that he had. Naturally he doesn't find it, as the boy claims he isn't dumb enough to keep it on him. He's told in response that he'll never make it to his new kris.

Elsewhere, Catherine is talking to Maria on the phone, and told of the miracle of the new kris for Tony. She goes on to explain that the kris will take place at eight o'clock that night, and emphasizes that the boy *must* be there at that time, or everything will be lost. Just as they hang up, Maria provides a warning about Vick, stating that the man will probably do anything he can to protect himself if he has something to lose. Understanding, Catherine then calls her apartment, but Tony doesn't answer. She goes home, finds the boy missing and proceeds to the auto body shop. It's night, and so she finds the place locked. Climbing a fence, she starts across the property, when a pair of Rottweilers come running at her. Diving into an old car, she slams the door shut just as the dogs slam against the window. The dogs continue their attack, until they start to break through the window. Suddenly Vincent, who stands atop the roof of the shop, leaps down. The dogs move in for the attack, but his stare is so "commanding," that they stop in mid-run, then whimper and lie down on the ground by his feet. He gets Catherine out of the car, with no further opposition from the animals.

Moving towards the padlocked building, Catherine calls out to Tony and they hear his muffled voice in response. Vincent smashes through the door, and the stunned boy merely stares at him. Catherine identifies him as a friend as she runs to Tony. It is Vincent's opinion that they will be able to move much faster underground, so that they will get to the kris on time.

Meanwhile, in a social hall, Vick is still trying to convince Milo that this new kris is wrong and a waste of time, but the older man refuses to listen to him. Unfortunately eight o'clock comes and goes, and Milo is about to cancel the kris, when the doors open and Tony runs in. The boy explains that Vick stole "the money" from the auto shop, and then framed his father, because without the boy's father standing in the way, Vick would be the next king of the Gypsies when Milo died. Vick, naturally, laughs this off, stating that he will not be accused by a ghost. Milo points out that the boy must have proof of this claim, or it will mean nothing. He says he has a letter of proof, and, as Catherine enters the room, he explains that he had placed it in her purse so that Vick would not be able to get his hands on it. Surprised, Catherine checks her purse and pulls out the letter. The document, reputedly written by Joe, is said to have been addressed to Tony's father, stating that he and Vick had stolen the money from the shop, and that he was afraid Vick would kill him for the rest of the money. Vick calls Joe a fool, but the latter states that he never wrote such a letter, and that "you said nobody could prove nothing." Milo looks at the paper, and finds that there are only a series of childish marks and scrawls on it, but no words. The old man tells Vick to read the letter that has condemned him, and the man is furious when he sees what it says.

"You were my son," says Milo simply, "but now you are no more. You walk in death."

Afterwards, Tony gives Milo the medallion we had seen earlier, and says that it came from Milo to his father and now back to the man so that he will have something to remember his son by. Milo, genuinely touched by the gesture, tells Tony that someday he will be able to give the medallion to his own son. Later, Tony thanks Catherine and asks her to pass his thanks on to Vincent.

When Catherine and Vincent are together, she explains that Tony stole a piece of her heart, to which he responds that the boy has taken a piece of hers with him. Staring deeply into his eyes, Catherine points out that Vincent helped her to find her way home, but he counters that they found the way together.

While "Everything is Everything" is by no means an outstanding episode, it is certainly an enjoyable one. Once again, it allows Catherine and Vincent to touch the lives of others, while enhancing their own relationship.

Episode Twenty

"To Reign in Hell"

Written by Howard Gordon and Alex Ganza

Directed by Christopher Leitch

Vincent is telling children the tale of Paracelsus, and via flashback, we hear a figure moving outside Catherine's window. We can see her through the panes of glass. Catherine feels the presence and believes it to be Vincent. She moves to step out to the terrace, while we intercut to the image of Vincent, who suddenly looks up, sensing the peril that she's in. Once outside Catherine is grabbed by what can only be described as an ogre-like human, who carries her to the tunnels beneath the city, to an area far beyond even that of Vincent and Father. In the meanwhile, Vincent has arrived at Catherine's apartment, only to find that she's not there. On the ground he sees a gold coin, which had come from Paracelsus' collection. Then he flashes back to his fight with the evil one, culminating in fire (all this told in flashback; for full details see the synopsis of "The Alchemist").

Back Underground, Vincent tells Father that Paracelsus is alive, and that he has taken Catherine somewhere, but somehow their bond has been broken. Father believes that if the man had intended to kill Catherine, he would have already done so. Instead, he's trying to lure Vincent away from this area, and Vincent will have to comply. Father acknowledges this, and points out that the madman probably believes that with Vincent out of the way, he will be able to rule the Underground. In addition, he adds that not only is Catherine's life at stake, but so is the whole future of the Underworld. Father tells Vincent to realize that with everything Paracelsus may say to him, there is a truth beyond knowledge.

There is much communication via the pipes, including what the community has termed a dead pipe. Winslow and another man try to follow it to the source, but it stops. They try listening with a stethoscope, and are able to decipher one word: Vincent. He arrives and is told that the pipe travels very far below, beyond even the wind tunnels. Perhaps three days travel, and one man, Pascal, believes that Paracelsus is the one who is sending the code. Winslow insists that he be brought along "for his own reasons." Vincent accepts this, and the three of them prepare for the long journey ahead of them.

Catherine awakens in Paracelsus' territory which could be a vision of hell itself, right down to the giant man that drags her some distance, until she meets the man himself, half his face covered in gold. He brings her a bowl of liquid and tells her to drink or else she will dehydrate. "You're certainly no use to me dead," he says simply. She wants to know why she's been brought there. He responds that Father had exiled him and this is his way of revenge, and Vincent is the only one standing between him and Father. Then he removes the gold plate from his face, revealing the terrible burns that have etched his face forever. This is something else he wishes to extract revenge for.

"I'm not afraid," says Catherine defiantly.

"You will be," he responds, adding that Vincent is coming to watch her die.

It's fine to be inspired by other genre films, but lifting two lines from **The Empire Strikes Back**? Remember the scene in question, when Luke Skywalker is about to enter a dark cavern and he tells Yoda that he isn't afraid? Well, Yoda leans forward and confidently says, "You will be."

Paracelsus tells his slave to make sure that Vincent continues his journey to this level alone.

Pascal tells his two companions that the tapping has stopped. What to do? The only thing they can: continue. They walk a little further and come across Narcissa (last seen in "Dark Spirit," and a very nice piece of continuity), and tell her the nature of their quest. She senses something about their quest, consults her magic stones and tells them to go back the way they came. She sees danger and death, but Vincent says that he must continue on the journey. Accepting this, Narcissa adds that Paracelsus has people of his own who follow and protect him; people who are "simple" and "lost" ones. Her words are chilling, but the trio nonetheless continue, making their way through the wind tunnels (and it must be pointed out that this set, coupled with an incredible matte painting, creates a completely fascinating and thoroughly realistic image of another world). They reach a fog covered pit, which has an extremely long rope/vine stretching down from the ceiling, and each makes their way down it, one by one.

They set up a fire for warmth, with Pascal talking about how he had once idolized Paracelsus, and how sad it is that the man has turned to evil. This said, he goes off to sleep, telling his two companions to awaken him when it's time for his shift. Once he's gone, Winslow asks Vincent what's on his mind, and he replies that he is concerned over his not being able to feel Catherine's fear. Winslow remembers when things were bad and people were desperate in the Underground, Paracelsus took advantage, his work convincing the people to follow him. But it was Father who had the wisdom and the strength to convince them that they were family and had to stand beside each other. After that Paracelsus was never the same, because he and Father had been friends, and now he felt betrayed. Winslow is about to go off to sleep, when he stops, turns around and explains that he's not just joining the search to get Paracelsus. It's also to help save Catherine, because she's a good woman and what is felt between Catherine and Vincent is something he himself has never felt. Watching them, he knows it's real and it allows him to believe in it. Several hours later, they continue.

They enter a cavern. Then Paracelsus' giant ogre-man steps out of the darkness, slams Pascal to the ground and is about to strike out at Winslow, when Vincent starts growling. The giant turns to face him, and knocks him down with his club. Then he slams Winslow against a wall. Vincent gets back to his feet and runs at him, but the giant gets the advantage, by slamming him against the ground. The giant moves towards Pascal for the kill, when an arrow strikes it in the back. Yelling in pain, it turns around to see the teenager Jamie, who had wanted to join the search but was denied by Vincent. She loads another arrow into her crossbow and fires it into the giant's shoulder. Vincent is then behind it. Suddenly the giant steps into the fog, and sinks out of sight. They rush over to examine Winslow, and Pascal makes the horrible announcement that Winslow is dead!

Winslow's death is significant to the series for one very important reason: it helps to create a greater sense of reality for the audience to hook on to. The idea is actually quite an intelligent one, because featuring this character in several episodes as one of the background players served to make the community of the Underworld much more believable. By killing him, we gain the sense that this is not just an extra biting the dust, but a valuable member of the world we've invested our emotions in.

Vincent, Pascal and Jamie share their memories of Winslow as they bury his body beneath stone. Jamie breaks down and starts crying, collapsing into Vincent's arms. Then Vincent decides that he must continue the journey alone, feeling that he is responsible for Winslow's death. Pascal points out that they came on their own, but Vincent still feels responsible. They, he says, should go back home to tell Father what has happened.

In Paracelsus' chamber, we see Catherine chained to a wall, with a the evil one stepping in and announcing that Vincent is close. Catherine says she knows this, causing Vincent to turn around and state that he's surprised she's not afraid to die. Catherine points out that it's sad the way he has lost everything he has worked to attain in his life. He doesn't agree, saying that he will reclaim what is rightfully his, and he will finally go home.

On a raft, Vincent is making his way across a vast Underground lake within a cavern, glancing from side to side as he makes passage. Finally he makes it to an "island" on the other side, and continues the search on foot. He is shocked to find the skeletal remains of someone chained to a wall, with the crystal he had given Catherine several episodes earlier hanging around its neck. This seems to renew his strength of purpose as he continues. He steps into another cavern, and hears Paracelsus' echoing voice: "Better to reign in hell, than to serve in heaven!"

Paracelsus steps out of the shadows, and is asked where Catherine is. He tells Vincent that she's well and alive for the moment, but if Vincent takes another step forward she will be killed. Paracelsus tells him that it was he who found Vincent as an infant and helped to raise him. The fact that he's alive has entirely to do with Paracelsus. It's obvious that Vincent does not believe him, as he won't allow the words to sway him as they almost did in "The Alchemist."

"What would you have me believe?" Vincent asks. "That you loved, and are now capable of this?"

Paracelsus says that this is the time for retribution. Again Vincent asks where Catherine is, and is told that she's in the pit directly below him. He leaps down, sees her chained to the wall and also the giant confronted earlier, who moves in for the kill. The fight between Vincent and the giant is ferocious with each gaining the upper hand and then losing it. The giant grabs Vincent in a bearhug and starts breaking his back, but Vincent claws the giant's back open, and then swings back and forth, opening up its neck. The giant collapses to the ground. Vincent frees Catherine, while Paracelsus leaves the chamber. By the time he and Catherine realize it, the man is long gone.

We dissolve to the image of Catherine and Vincent rafting their way back home. He hands her crystal back to her and explains that for the first time she felt distant to him. She said she was afraid, but she couldn't let her fear control her. Catherine mentions the past that Paracelsus spoke of, but Vincent counters that Father's words from before are now clear to him: behind knowledge there is truth, and now Vincent realizes that that truth is love.

"To Reign in Hell" is one of the best episodes of **Beauty and the Beast**'s first season, and one of the most unusual. This is probably the closest to the original fairy tale that this show has come, and yet it is coupled with a fantasy element which can't help but evoke J.R.R. Tolkien's **The Lord of the Rings** trilogy, right down to the fellowship going off on a sacred quest and the battle between good and evil. Undoubtedly one of the most significant elements of this story is that it serves as proof positive that **Beauty and the Beast** can work as either a humanistic action/adventure show on the surface of the city, or a fantasy in the Underground.

Episode Twenty One

"Ozmandias"

Written by George R.R. Martin

Directed by Frank Beascoechea

An opening montage paints a succinct image of the differences between the surface and the Underworld, as the foundation for a new skyscraper is being laid down, while we are witness to the beauty of the world which lies beneath the ground.

Meanwhile, at the DA's office, a meeting is in progress between DA Moreno, Joe Maxwell, Catherine, Elliot Burch (who we've seen twice already in the course of the series) and his lawyer, Roth, who is pointing out that the DA's office owes Burch something for his testifying against Max Avery. It is his opinion that something be done about Luz Corrales, to which Catherine responds that she didn't know it was against the law to oppose Burch. Moreno says he has to agree with her. Finally, Burch asks Roth to leave the room, which the man reluctantly does. Once the man is gone, Burch explains that he recognizes the fact that many people aren't happy with Burch Tower, but Luz is resorting to sabotage, harassment and the theft of equipment, and Avery is doing his best to help bring Burch down, just as Elliot's testimony did him. Moreno says that the DA's office will investigate and do what they can. He thanks them and leaves the office, followed by Catherine. She quickly explains that she's not his enemy, only that she's against the idea of Burch Tower. He'd like the opportunity to change her mind, but she doesn't see the point of it, as the tower will go up whether she approves of it or not. When he agrees with this, Catherine replies that she'll listen to what he has to say.

In the Underground, we see paintings of the past, including one of an infant Vincent being held by a much younger Father. Vincent is looking at the artwork with Catherine, explaining that somehow they touch on the surface as well as the tunnel realm.

"Someday," he muses, "when all of us are gone...your world will find these painted tunnels...wonder at them, cherish them...and remember, in some small way, the lives we led...the dreams we dreamt..."

Vincent goes on to explain that Elizabeth, the artist, has lived in the Underground even longer than Father has, and that she still remains something of an enigma to all of them. They know virtually nothing of her past. Catherine points out that the woman speaks through her brush. Their conversation is suddenly interrupted by the sounds of explosions overhead, which cause the tunnels to shake in response. Once the shaking subsides, Vincent points out that the explosions have been taking place for several weeks, and are growing ever closer. He mentions a tower that "sinks its roots deep into the earth...deeper than any building has ever gone before." Catherine realizes that this is the Burch Tower that Vincent is speaking of, and she can feel his pain as he explains that Father believes that the tower could mean the end of their world.

Now while all of this is fine and dandy, one must ask a question: if this is such a serious threat, why is Vincent being so casual about it? If, as he has explained, the explosions have been going on for several weeks, then why hasn't something been said to Catherine sooner? How can he possibly come across as so calm?

That night, Catherine shows up at Elliot's office, and is a bit surprised to discover that Burch Tower is going to cost some three *billion* dollars. This, of course, doesn't bother Elliot, who goes on to explain that this project will represent a dream come true for him. As he speaks, Catherine can feel the man's passion for this particular dream, and rapidly comes to the horrible conclusion that there probably won't be a single thing she can do to stop the construction of Burch Tower.

Underground Vincent approaches Elizabeth, who is in the midst of yet another tunnel painting. He tries to convince her to move to the lower levels, pointing to the explosions above as the reason. She refuses, pointing out that her life is on these particular walls, and when they are gone, so shall she be. Vincent seems to appreciate her words. Later, in Vincent's chamber, Father voices his concern that the tower will expose four to six levels of the Underground, and that there really is no way for them to minimize their exposure to the surface world. Relocation, it would seem, would be the only solution, but there is no way to relocate Elizabeth—she will not be moved. Mouse, who is also there, details a plan he has come up with which will guide an Underground river in such a way as to flood the foundation, and therefore the construction crews will have no choice but to stop their work. Father, who has proven that he can be something of a pessimist, states that the number of man-hours necessary for such a task would be staggering. Mouse agrees, voicing his opinion that they had best get started then. Again, Father says it's impossible, and Vincent agrees with him. Hurt and angry, Mouse snaps, "You let Winslow die. Now Elizabeth!" He leaves the chamber.

On the surface Catherine decides to meet with Luz Corrales, who she had known in the past but hasn't seen in quite some time. Meanwhile Underground, Mouse is talking to Elizabeth, when another explosion sends rubble down that nearly crushes them, and which succeeds in damaging some of her tunnel paintings. Furious, Elizabeth states that she's going to have to paint the pictures all over again. Genuinely touched by her pain, Mouse replies that he's going to stop the explosions and that everything will be okay again.

That evening, Luz Corrales, who is working with public support groups, shows up at Catherine's apartment. Their conversation eventually turns to the Burch Tower, which Corrales is dead set against, believing that it will do more harm than good to the neighborhood. She plans on opposing it by taking Burch himself to court in a class action suit. Catherine makes note of some of the donations which have reached Corrales' people, adding that it may be coming from Max Avery. The implication of "dirty" money infuriates the woman, who starts to walk out of the apartment. Then she stops, turns to Catherine and says that she will look into that possibility. "I don't like to be used," she snaps, as she walks out.

Underground Father is fearful that moving to the lower levels will cost them everything they've built. They will be below the areas of pipes where communication will be cut off. Vincent believes that they will be able to rebuild whatever they lose, and that their world, no matter what, *will* survive. Elizabeth suddenly arrives, telling them that she's worried about Mouse, who has gone above to do something about the blasting that it taking place. Vincent, panic-stricken, runs off.

Mouse arrives at the construction site, having crawled out of a drainage pipe. He carefully eludes a security guard, but is captured by several others. Vincent watches in terror as the boy is shoved towards a trailer by the guards. Inside he is questioned by them, but refuses to answer. The men remove the items from his pouch and find plastic explosives. Elliot is called, and he is absolutely furious, but he hangs up when Catherine, who has been made aware of the situation, arrives at his office. She tells him that the apprehended boy may have a case of false imprisonment against Burch. Elliot won't buy this, wanting to know why the boy asked for Catherine by name, but couldn't tell them the name of the President of the United States.

She merely asks that he let him go, but he wants to know what is going on. Catherine, on the other hand, explains that she can't provide any explanations because of a promise she had made. He considers her words.

Underground Father, feeling guilty for what has happened to Mouse, explains that they will have to somehow raise the bail money to get the boy freed. They will have to go to their helpers on the surface. Vincent remains convinced that Catherine will help them. At that moment, she steps out of the shadows, followed by Mouse. Father insists that it's time he and the boy had a long talk. As they leave the chamber, Catherine tells Vincent that she is completely indebted to Elliot for the help that he provided her *and* the Underground in the past. How can she possibly destroy his dream? Vincent replies that she can't, and that the people of the Underground have no right to ask her to do so. It remains nonetheless obvious that this thought tortures Vincent, as does the image of what the Burch Tower will do to his people.

When Catherine arrives home, she is surprised to find Elliot awaiting her in the hallway. He asks if he can come in for some coffee. She responds in the affirmative. After some hesitation, Elliot makes the announcement: he's in love with her. Although Catherine tries to dissuade him from these feelings, he ultimately asks her to marry him. He asks her to at least consider his proposal, adding that he would do anything to make her happy.

The next day, at work, Catherine is considering everything that is happening, when Luz enters her office and slams a newspaper on the desk. Its headline screams: "DA Probes Corrales Group." Catherine denies any knowledge of this, but Luz refuses to believe her. This story has cost her the battle against Burch Tower. Joe Maxwell approaches, pointing out that over seventy contributors to her organization have ties with Max Avery. She leaves the building, and Catherine asks for the rest of the day off. She goes to the tunnels, where she tells Vincent that there is no other choice. She is going to have to marry Elliot Burch, because Luz, the only potential obstacle standing in the tower's way, is no longer a threat. Vincent cannot accept this, pointing out that she does not love this man. Catherine counters that there is much more at stake than just her happiness. What she does or does not do might determine the destiny of what happens to all the people of the Underground. In her mind, there is no choice. She goes to Elliot's office, tells him that she'll marry him and he kisses her passionately. Then she drops the bombshell: she wants him to stop construction of the tower. Elliot is stunned, explaining that he wants the two of them to live on the top floor so that they can overlook the entire city. He says that he can't stop the construction. Catherine replies that she understands and leaves him alone in his very large office.

Yet another bombshell is dropped the next day at the DA's office, when Catherine is told that Avery couldn't possibly have had anything to do with Luz and the people opposed to the tower, because his assets were frozen. Then the horrible realization hits her: Elliot is the one who has "tainted" Luz's image and instigated the current investigation. Later, she goes to the Underground and tells Vincent how painful her being willing to marry Elliot was. He points out that she was nonetheless able to help everyone.

We see Elizabeth painting, Elliot staring into the Manhattan skyline, and a newspaper headline which reads: "Court Blocks Burch Tower," in rapid succession.

Once again, a terrific episode, with plenty of pathos and believable characterizations.

Never before has exposure of the Underworld seemed so imminent, and the danger so tangible.

Elliot Burch remains a fascinating guest star, although one would think that there would be little more use for him in future episodes. Still, like Paracelsus, it is conceivable that this Donald Trump-like character will reappear.

The scenes with Elizabeth, incidentally, are truly wonderful, and help to sustain the magic of the Underground.

Episode Twenty Two

"A Happy Life"

Written by Ron Koslow

Directed by Victor Lobl

Catherine is dreaming of her childhood, and of her mother. She awakens in bed and starts to cry, but pulls herself together to call her office and tells them that she won't be in. Later, her father shows up at the apartment, and the two talk about the arrival of the twentieth anniversary of Catherine's mother's death. She says that it all hit her this morning, the memory being stronger than it had ever been before. Her father, of course, can identify with what she's feeling. When asked, he tells Catherine that all her mother had wanted for her was a happy life. This said, he invites her out for lunch, but she has to decline, having promised to have lunch with an old friend named Nancy Tucker, who's in for West Port with her two children. "She's having a happy life," says Catherine.

At lunch, Nancy invites her to spend some time at West Port, and tells her to bring someone with her if she likes. Catherine says that her relationship is a little bit hard to explain. "If he makes you happy," offers Nancy, "then that's all that matters."

That night on her terrace, Catherine flashes back to being tucked in by her mother. Flashback ended, we find that she's talking to Vincent, explaining that she was ten years old when her mother died. Today, more than ever, she's feeling an incredible feeling of loss, not just for her mother, but for a part of her life as well. For the lost safety and simplicity, which she saw in her friend's face. Vincent suggests that these feelings are calling out to remind her of something that she needs, of what she longs for. He says that the memory of her mother reminds Catherine of her aloneness, and of the family that was lost when she died, as well as of all the friends she lost when she and Vincent met. The secret she carries sets her apart from her past and everyone else that she knows. Her family, her friends, the children waiting to be born. "Our dream exists," he says, "at the cost of all your other dreams. Know that, Catherine." She says it's worth it, but we can tell that Vincent isn't quite so sure it's right for her.

The next day at work, Catherine is given a heavy workload, which we can see she's not really up to. Later that day, she goes to see a psychiatrist, and tries to get a handle on her problem. She tells the doctor of her feeling regarding the anniversary of her mother's death, and the hopelessness she feels in life. He wants to know if her feelings have anything to do with the attack on her over a year ago. She gets angry at this suggestion, saying that she's there to reconcile her feelings regarding her mother's death. Finally she starts talking about the relationship she's involved in, passing Vincent off as a human male so that they can discuss it. Hearing the frustration she's feeling, the doctor asks if she wants to end the relationship, but she says she doesn't. He's befuddled by her claim that this Vincent gives her everything she's ever needed. The psychiatrist wants to know what the problem is then. Catherine explains that a part of her wants to live with him in his world, and the other part is a woman trying to have a life in New York, which is an impossible feeling to deal with.

Vincent sits silently with Father, his mind distracted from the game of chess they're in the midst of playing. Father asks what's troubling him, even though he knows the answer before the question is asked. Vincent says that Catherine is in great turmoil, and this has put him in a sour mood. Father admires his courage, but Vincent points out that Catherine has the same amount of courage, to try to fight impossible odds for their love. Father says he will pray for both of them.

Catherine receives a phone call from Nancy, who invites her up to West Point the following Friday. She says she'll try to make it. Next day, Joe comes to Catherine's office saying that she did the wrong case breakdown, which is as shocking to her as it is to Joe. Back at the psychiatrist's office, Catherine talks about Vincent overcoming incredible pain with the most beautiful heart she's ever known. The doctor suggests that this can't be very fulfilling, but she argues that that's the only part of her life that is fulfilling. The doctor says that to help her, he must know more of this Vincent, but she says she can't break her promise to Vincent.

Back at work, Catherine tells Joe she's going to have to take some time off, which he at first refuses to allow. She responds by telling him that she's going to have to quit for personal reasons, but he tells her to make it personal time; that she shouldn't quit. "You work yourself too hard," he says sincerely, "but I take advantage." He says he owes her, and offers any help he can give.

Catherine meets her father and his date for a concert, where she tells him that she's going to take some time off to go to West Point and drive through New England. This delights him. The concert begins, and Catherine's joy turns to sadness as she starts to cry, and has to excuse herself. She runs to the park and the tunnel entrance, where Vincent is waiting for her, having felt that she would be coming this way. Crying, she tells him that the pianist was playing the music they had heard one night under the park, and all she could think of was that she wanted him there to hear it with her. It almost became physically painful, so she had to run from it. What are they to do before there's nothing left for either of them.

Vincent points out that this was the risk they faced, and now perhaps they should awaken from their dream and return to their lives. Catherine says she wants to come below, to try to live with his people. As much as the words pain him, he says that she has a life above, and to turn her back on that would be the same as turning her back on who she is and what she is destined to become. Then, she asks, what should she do? Maybe if she just went away for a while, it would help. Vincent states that their relationship must end, because he cannot bear the pain he is causing her; the mocking of their dreams that he is the cause of. He suggests that she use the depths of their love to provide the courage to allow her to love someone else. Sadly, he retreats further into the tunnels, closing the passage, and effectively blocking Catherine's entrance to the Underworld. Crying, she leaves.

The next day, Catherine calls Nancy and tells her that she's coming up a little early, and will be arriving by train that night. Vincent, a tear running down his face, feels that she is leaving. Once she's arrived in West Point, Catherine gets the taste of life on the other side of the fence, if you will, as she gathers with a group of old friends, all of whom, except for her, are with a husband or boyfriend. The one free male, the brother of her friend Rebecca, asks Catherine if she would like to spend some time together the next day. She suggests they talk about it the next day.

Vincent arrives at Catherine's apartment, and flashes back to the night he gave her the crystal necklace, as well as other nights, as he allows the memories to wash over him. At the same time, Catherine is having a dream that the she and Vincent are walking the surface world without fear. He asks how this could be, and her response is that it's what she has wished for, more than anything. They proclaim their love for each other and are about to kiss, when Catherine is startled to see that Rebecca's brother is sitting next to her, with the figure of Vincent walking away. She calls out to him, but he doesn't turn around. Catherine is suddenly awake in bed, sobbing. Later, she's talking to Nancy, wondering if her relationship with Vincent can ever result in a normal life. Nancy points out that marriage and children isn't always everything that you would hope it would be; that there will always be a downside to everything. Everyone is proud of Catherine's accomplishments, but the only advice she can offer Catherine is to follow her heart. Catherine smiles, as this is what Vincent always tells her. Nancy wants to know if they'll ever meet Vincent, and Catherine smiles, saying that she's beginning to believe that anything is possible. She borrows the woman's car and starts driving back to New York.

Vincent sits alone, staring into a waterfall, obviously lost in thought over Catherine. Suddenly he is aware of the joy that Catherine is now feeling, and the fact that she's coming back to the city. He bolts from the chamber he was sitting in. She drives as he races through the tunnels (one can only assume that he was very far from his usual area). He leaves the entrance of the tunnel just as Catherine is running towards him. They hug each other passionately, with Catherine asking that he forgive her for doubting their love was strong enough to conquer this fear. "What we have is all that matters," she says. "It's worth everything."

They stare into each other's eyes and are about to move in for the oft-promised kiss, but then the frame freezes, as silhouettes continue the journey behind them and kiss passionately, symbolic, no doubt, of the union between their spirits.

Despite a cop-out of a final image, "A Happy Life" is another episodes which assures there is not a dry eye in the living room. The story is an important one, forcing Catherine and Vincent to look at the downside of their relationship and come to grips with what exists between them. And perhaps with the understanding of the limitations of what can exist in the future.

The message is simple: love conquers all. **Beauty and the Beast** could not end its first season on a more appropriate note.

SECOND SEASON

Perhaps the greatest attribute of **Beauty and the Beast**'s first season was its uncanny ability to deal with the Vincent/Catherine romance, while using it as subtext to humanistic dramas that alternated between both of their worlds. Catherine and Vincent loved each other, there was no doubt about that, but their love—despite pervading just about every scene—was never so overwhelming that the viewer felt that that was all there was to the show.

The same cannot be said for the second season.

Unfortunately, the powers-that-be apparently examined the fan mail and cult following the series had garnered, and came to the conclusion that the relationship between the principles was the most appealing aspect of the show, and thus decided to focus on that. While the majority of episodes still dealt with Catherine and Vincent interacting with others, there was a subtle alteration of the formula. First off, most of the episodes seemed to take place Underground, which is fascinating, but can't help but get repetitive week after week. Plus a primary emphasis was placed on our hero and heroine looking longingly at each other, speaking breathlessly, quoting poetry and wishing they could be together for all eternity.

As touching as much of this was, it seemed as though **Beauty and the Beast** was becoming "Thirtysomething With Fur," and the audience began tuning out in droves. Ratings plummeted. The series, which had been scoring in the 40s on the rating charts during season one, suddenly dropped into the Neilson basement, and the rumor began that third year renewal was growing dimmer. The creative staff tried to examine the situation, seemed to recognize that Vincent was not "Hulking out" enough, and not fighting off those who would prey on the innocent with his fangs, claws and growls. As a result, they went in the extreme opposite direction. Suddenly Vincent was back to his old ways, but it seemed like he was attacking and killing perpetrators during the first five minutes of every episode. This beast was suddenly unchained, and that, too, left an unpleasant taste in the audience's mouth.

Now the show is fighting for its life, with CBS okaying 12 episodes which are considered make-or-break in terms of the series' continued survival. The rumor is that those episodes, which are scheduled to air in early 1990, will take the show in very different directions.

A prelude to those directions was found in the final "trilogy" of the second season, which explored the characters, particularly Vincent, in minute detail and provided an incredible wealth of background. Because of the significance of these revelations, this section of the revised edition will look at these three episodes.

PART I:

At night Catherine is walking through the park towards the tunnel entrance to the Underworld, when she is approached and attacked by two police officers. Vincent leaps out of the darkness, and quickly disposes of them. He runs to her side, and the two proceed Underground, where they try to reason out what just happened.

Later, on the surface, police have arrived, including a reporter named Bernie Spurko. Still later we see Spurko at work on his story, and it's obvious that he's investigating these attacks which seem to have been committed by an animal.

Next night, Spurko is in a penthouse and is told to sit by a shadowy figure, whose voice sounds like Elliot Burch. We learn that he is the one who sent the fake police officers out to intercept Catherine in the park, and then he details the pattern of killings that started two years earlier. People were attacked by this creature and left to bleed to death. He then identifies Catherine Chandler as the creature's object of affection. The following morning, Spurko shows up at the DA's office and tries questioning Catherine, but she claims she doesn't know anything. He proceeds to discuss various cases (which were part of previous episodes), pointing out the pattern of murders.

Meanwhile Underground, Father tells Catherine that the risk of discovery is growing each time Catherine and Vincent see each other, although she shouldn't blame herself. Perhaps, she suggests, she's been reckless, putting herself in danger because she knows Vincent will be there to help. Later, she meets with Vincent, who has already been informed of Spurko's questions by father. They enjoy the comfort of each other beneath the park, listening to a concert.

Meanwhile, Spurko goes to the mental institution where Stephen Bass ("Down to a Sunless Sea") resides. He thinks that Catherine still loves him, and through flashbacks recalls the night that Vincent confronted him. He remembers that she had referred to the creature as Vincent, and then shows off his scars received during the attack.

At his newspaper, Spurko hands his story in, but can't attribute much of it because, even though he knows his source is Elliot Burch, he can't reveal that in print. The editor says the only way the story is going to be printed is if Burch comes forward.

Next day, Spurko sees Catherine in the streets, and starts questioning her about Stephen Bass, even playing back some of the tape. Distraught, she walks away from him.

Underground Father is in the midst of a conversation with Vincent, trying to console him. Vincent is starting to question his very identity. He feels the animal side of him is in struggle with his humanity.

Meanwhile, Catherine does some research on Spurko, and finds that Burch had leaked a story to the reporter a year earlier. She confronts Burch with this, but he denies any knowledge of Spurko's investigating her or Vincent. From there, she goes to the tunnel world and tells Vincent that Burch has been leaking information, and that the reporter got to Stephen Bass. Catherine feels that maybe they shouldn't see each other for a while, for the risk is too great. Vincent's feelings of inadequacy and of being different start to overwhelm him.

Given yet another tip, Spurko goes to the underground beneath Catherine's building. Above, two men kill the building's maintenance manager, and go up to her apartment, where they break in, tape up her mouth and drag her down to the basement, and then beneath it. As they abuse her physically, Vincent bursts through a wall, and claws them to death. Spurko stands there, snapping photographs. Vincent turns to him, and he screams out in fear, practically breaking down and crying. Vincent stops himself at the last moment, and nearly collapses against a wall, before retreating into the tunnels. Recomposing himself, Spurko says that his story will indeed run, and he leaves.

Catherine goes into the tunnel after Vincent, but he tells her to go; that they must end their relationship, because when this story is published, the people above will hound him until he's dead. A final embrace and she's gone, sobbing.

Spurko goes back to the penthouse demanding all the information Burch has, because the man has a lot to answer for, such as the deaths of two innocent men. Burch states that it would have been better if Spurko had not learned quite so much. Suddenly Burch steps out of the shadows, revealing himself to be Paracelsus. Explaining his impersonation of Burch as a "trick of the throat," he approaches and notes that what Spurko saw tonight was glorious. Vincent, he adds, is above being a man; he is a God, but in trying to be a man he denies his own greatness. According to Paracelsus, Vincent is a killer, and that is the source of his greatness. Then, he approaches the reporter, emits his wrist blade and says, "It's too bad he didn't kill you tonight, as I thought he would. If he had killed an innocent man, he would have finally understood and shed the false skin of his humanity; he would have become what I always dreamed of him...he would have become my son." He swiftly guts the man.

Vincent's descent into madness continues, as he paces his chamber like a caged animal.

PART II:

Catherine awakens from a nightmare in which Spurko's story has been printed, and she is being hounded by the media and the public.

Underground Vincent stands before a a river, staring at his reflection. Father approaches, stating that it's been four days and the story has not appeared in the newspaper. Perhaps this reporter had a change of heart, and decided not to print his article. Vincent is distraught, stating that as long as he and Catherine are involved with each other, there will always be someone with a camera or a notepad.

Father states, "What you have with Catherine is a wonderful dream, but this is your home."

"No, Father," he responds sadly. "This is my tomb."

At work, Catherine is shown the day's newspaper by Joe, who explains that Spurko's body has been found, and that he was killed by a double-edged blade, similar to a surgical tool. Meanwhile, Burch wants to know who was giving Spurko information and why this person was trying to impersonate him. His spy sets off to find answers.

Father receives an envelope containing photos of Vincent, with a note telling him to come alone to the penthouse. He instinctively knows that this is from Paracelsus. Father dresses for the surface world, takes a gun and goes to the appointed place. There he meets Parcelsus, stating that he won't allow the photos to be published. He pulls out the gun, but is unable to pull the trigger. When asked what he wants, Paracelsus responds that it's time for Vincent to claim his birthright, and he pulls out a locket.

Catherine comes home to find Father waiting for her in the hall, holding a locket which contains the photo of a woman. They go to the Underground, where Father explains that the woman's name was Anna. He tells a tale of this woman who loved to walk the surface, and Vincent asks if she's the one who found him. Seeming somewhat reluctant, Father says that he was never found; that was only a story. Anna was actually his mother. Vincent is stunned, wanting to know what happened to her, and is told that she died, and is buried in the catacombs. In anger, Vincent leaves the chamber and Catherine tries to follow him.

Burch's spy tells him that Spurko had illegally parked in front of the building with the penthouse, which has no name on the lease. The leaser paid twice the yearly rent in gold. Burch states that he wants full monitoring systems, including phone taps, installed.

Vincent wants to be alone, but Catherine wants desperately to help him. This, he feels, is something that he must confront alone, and he goes off to the catacombs where he sees Narcissa, and Anna's tomb. There he discovers that Anna was actually married to Paracelsus, which would make Paracelsus his father.

Vincent returns to Father's chamber and tells Catherine to leave, which she does. He confronts Father with his discovery. Father explains that Paracelsus and Anna had tried to have a child, but that he couldn't father a child. Through medical experimentation he had made her pregnant, but she went into labor during her third month. Vincent is horrified to learn that he was not born like other children. Instead, he ripped his way out of his mother's body, killing her.

Devastated, Vincent returns to his chamber, where Catherine awaits him. He tells her to leave this world and return to her own and the life she had. She says she's a part of him, and tries to make him see the goodness in his soul. "It is not safe to love me," he says. "I killed Anna. These hands ripped apart my mother's flesh; I was born in blood." She tries to embrace him, but he merely growls in response. She leaves.

Catherine is told by Elliot Burch that they found the penthouse, and invites her along. There they find a hollow wall and a hidden passage, within which lies a bound Father, stating that Paracelsus has gone below.

Underground the real Father explains to Catherine that Anna lost her baby in the third month and shortly afterward found Vincent above. Things then became confused in Paracelsus' mind, and when she gave the child to Father for safekeeping, Paracelsus poisoned her.

Meanwhile, Father/Paracelsus is with Vincent, who wants to know why he let him live. He claims that he knew Vincent was something new that had come into the world, but Vincent wants to know how Father could manipulate and lie to so many people. They, according to Father, were not important. Only Vincent was. Their confrontation grows, along with Vincent's anger. Father encourages feelings of anger and hatred, resulting in Vincent delivering a death blow. Before dying, Father reveals himself to be Paracelsus.

"At last," he says weakly, "you are my son."

Catherine and the real Father arrive, and some time later Catherine notes that the nightmare is finally over. "No," he says simply. "It's not over."

PART III:

Vincent runs through the park toward Catherine. When a group of police officers are horseback surround him, they start emptying their weapons into his body. He collapses to the ground, staring at Catherine's completely unemotional face.

Naturally this is a dream, but when he awakens it is in the park, and the sun is out. He barely manages to return to the sanctuary of the tunnel without being seen. He tells Father, and then when Catherine arrives later on, she wants nothing but to help, and he refuses. He goes back to his chamber, not understanding the madness in himself.

Catherine sees Father and tries to gain answers. He explains that Vincent's entire life has been a series of balances, and now that balance has been disturbed by recent events. He goes on to explain that this happened once in Vincent's adolescence, and he had to be restrained because all attempts at sedation failed.

Later, Vincent tries to calm himself by reading, but it's obvious he's quickly losing his grip. That evening he goes to Catherine's apartment, but she is not home. Growing impatient, he smashes through the glass doors and tears the place apart, before slipping into unconsciousness. Catherine return home to find him there, and slowly tries nursing him back to health, much as he did her in the original series pilot. Eventually it seems as though her treatment is working, but this is short-lived. He returns to the Underground, and almost immediately finds himself losing the balance Father had spoken of.

The Tunnel-Dwellers put up barriers so Vincent can't leave, which infuriates him. Father tries to calm him, and nearly receives a death blow for his troubles.

Ultimately, Vincent retreats to a cave, where he emits sounds like those of a wounded and furious animal. Catherine arrives and wants to see him, but Father resists. "He's my life, Father," she screams out. "I must go to him."

She proceeds into the cave. The howls intensify and she screams out Vincent's name....

FADE TO BLACK.

The season's over.

Needless to say, these three episodes were one hell of a way to end the season. The plot twists were dynamic (if not repetitive of the Darth Vader/ Luke Skywalker father-son plotline of **Star Wars**), and Paracelsus truly revealed himself in many ways to be Vincent's dark side. Also, the dark side of this noble lion-man has always been hinted at, it was never before explored in depth. The audience hopes Vincent will come to grips with what's happening to him and regains his "balance."

Linda Perlman is pregnant in real life, and will be written out of future episodes. She will be replaced by another actress.

Whatever the outcome of season two's trilogy and the various rumors surrounding the show's return, one can only hope Beauty and the Beast will return to the greatness of its first season, and recapture the magic it once had.

The HERO and the VILLAIN

The Hero

"I think Vincent is the Prince, and I think the job that Rick Baker has done, and the job that the writers have done and the job that I'm trying to do, bears that out in every episode," exclaims actor Ron Perlman. "He is the most sublime thing in Catherine Chandler's life. He doesn't need to change—to become that Prince—to be accepted by her. That's how we get around the transformation. There's no reason to see this guy change, because he's as close to perfect as you're going to get. There's a lot to be said for people who ask, 'How the hell are we going to sustain this for 22 weeks a year for the next five years?' That's the exercise, and every week we address that exercise with various degrees of success. We've already put some wonderful episodes on the air, and as long as we can do that, and as long as the writers stay as fertile as they've been, then the question will be answered as we go along."

Perlman is speaking of the final moments of the original tale of Beauty and the Beast, as well as the classic Jean Cocteau film of the same name, in which the love of beauty transforms the homely, but noble, beast into a handsome Prince. He is also referring to the CBS weekly series, at the time of writing still preparing for 12 "make-or-break" episodes in terms of the show's survival. The series casts Perlman as Vincent, the lion-man who resides in New York's Underworld, and Linda Hamilton as the aforementioned attorney, Catherine Chandler. The two of them were brought together by chance (though some would say it was more the hand of destiny), and developed an eternal, albeit unconsummated, love for each other. It is their passion that drives the series forward week after week.

"It's so romantic," Perlman enthuses, "and it's not really very science fiction or fantasy oriented. It's very real. They've found very contemporary equivalents to the magical and fanciful elements, certainly, but in a very real setting. It's real easy to suspend your disbelief, which is one of the things that I have discovered working on it. The benefits of playing Vincent are incredible. There are elements that one has to come to grips with in terms of Vincent's character, which are so elevated, noble and regal, you can't help but get involved. He's so spiritual, so sensitive to the world and humanity around him, that I've begun looking at the world through his eyes, because I spend so many hours of my day walking in his shoes.

"I'm not going to say that I become Vincent," he adds. "I don't want you to interpret this in that way, but the only thing an actor has as his tools is his own experience, and you have to find things in you to play that the character in the script calls for. Insofar as I've been doing that to the degree I have been, yes, I've become very intimately involved in what I have in me that's similar to Vincent. One of the turn-ons of being an actor is being given the opportunity to occasionally be more than you are, or less than you are. It certainly takes you out of the realm of being yourself."

Perlman, who has seemingly made a career for himself as an actor who dons prosthetics, feels that there is a significant difference between Vincent and some of his earlier roles in such films as **Quest for Fire** and **The Name of the Rose**, in which he portrayed, respectively, a prehistoric caveman and a disfigured monk.

"The humanity of those two people was so abstract that I had to form a new level of behavior," he explains. "A new walk, a new voice, a new language, new places that the language comes from...those are all intellectual decisions and inventive decisions. Vincent needs to be played right from the heart. What state his emotions are in at any given moment dictates how he is to be played. Not invention, not imagination or any of those things. Just purely using the scripts as a guideline to what is needed emotionally in any given situation. It's a different type of acting than I've ever had to do. I'm really enjoying it because it's very honest and simple; it's the kind of thing I've been hoping for. It's a role that associates a romantic leading character with a character actor. I play both now, and Vincent, aside from the fact that he is so physically different, is definitely a romantic hero."

Indeed, Vincent's romantic appeal is being registered all across the country, as women of all ages find themselves drawn to his nobility of spirit. In fact, much as has been the case with the character of Star Trek's Mr. Spock over the past two decades, the physical and emotional differences between Vincent and everyone else has led to a large degree of fantasy among the show's distaff fans. Many of them forward rather suggestive letters to the actor. But what is the phenomenal appeal of this character?

"First of all," responds Perlman, "there's not a character around that I've come into contact with who possesses as much humility as he does. That humility serves as a backdrop to his other qualities, which are incredible strength, both spiritual and physical and an innate leadership quality based on his solitude and aloneness and good judgement, as well as his compassion for the underdog. Those who have been dealt a few cards less in the big deal. Certainly he has been, and his compassion makes him a sort of Albert Sweitzer. He's achieved a sort of self actualization in is own life and he's very, very secure in what he is and who he is. In fact, he's so secure that he is able to begin to live for the world around him rather than for himself. A character like that is very rare in life. There are those people out there, but they're usually Nobel Peace Prize winners. Those are the things I see in Vincent, and those are the things I try to put into the playing of him that people are responding to."

Perlman himself responded immediately to the role. He had appeared in a number of feature films and stage productions, and attained perhaps the most attention for his role in **The Name of the Rose**, which, he feels, was indirectly responsible for his being cast as Vincent.

"My version of it is probably a lot different from other people's versions," Perlman laughs, "but at the time they were conceptualizing this series, **The Name of the Rose** had been released. 20th Century Fox, the film's distributor, mounted a modest Oscar nomination campaign on my behalf, so I was very prominent in the press and I got real good reviews for the performance. I guess my name went on that list of guys who do well in prosthetics, and they submitted my name to the show. Rick Baker, who was designing Vincent's make-up, went heavily to bat for me, because he knew the films I had been in and knew that I would be used to the battle that would have to be fought in getting the make-up on every day. Then I went in and read, and my empathy for the character and the script was, I guess, apparent and, from what I understand, I really didn't have much competition once I read. When I went to read for the network, I had only read the script twice because I didn't want to mess with it. Usually you spend weeks getting into a character, but Vincent I just wanted to leave as an extension of my first instinct of what he was, because that was so clear to me. It was an immediate response, which is how fleshed out I thought the character was in the script, which is really a tribute to Ron Koslow's writing.

"I had played beasts prior to this, but this was not only a beast, but a beast who lived as an extension of his pain every moment of every day. All of that was there in the relationship with this woman who opened up all of these new feelings in him. It was just mind-blowing that somebody could come up with a character that crystalized all of the beasts that had ever been written in history, including the Hunchback of Notre Dame, the beast from the Cocteau film and the beast that I played in **Name of the Rose**. These guys, I always felt, had tremendous feelings underneath their ugliness and those things were always touched on by the other characterizations, but never as articulately or as fleshed out as in this version. I saw an incredible sensitivity on the part of the writer for this man's pain, and yet his ability to transcend that pain."

Despite prior statements to the contrary, Perlman ultimately decided to go ahead with yet another role which required a heavy amount of make-up, but this was different from all others in that it has been a daily, and sometimes grueling, experience. And yet that aspect of playing Vincent doesn't seem to bother him, as the benefits of playing the character are stronger than any of the drawbacks.

"Make-up has always been rather freeing for me," Perlman admits. "When you're playing a character, you're playing someone other than yourself, and when you physically put something on that makes you look like somebody else, then it frees you to be that person, rather than being incumbered by the limitations of what you look like. It is, however, something of a nuisance to be sitting in a chair four hours every day to get made up, and then for an hour to get the make-up taken off. So that's five hours added on to whatever kind of shooting day we have, and that's been averaging about twelve or fourteen hours. I have had more than my fair share of twenty hour days. Now that we have been doing this for quite a while, it's been a real test of my endurance. So far the incredible excitement I have for just getting to play this character who's so much larger than life, so incredible, far outweighs the negatives. It's the most beautiful character I've ever played, and maybe that I ever will. He's a combination of Hamlet, Superman and the Cocteau beast. Maybe I never will get tired of it, no matter what the problems are."

As stated previously, the thrust behind **Beauty and the Beast** is the Vincent/Catherine romance, and as one watches the on-screen sparks between the two characters, the question of what the Perlman/Hamilton relationship is like arises. As does the inevitable inquiry as to when the on-screen duo will consummate their relationship, if ever.

"I truly believe the chemistry between Linda and myself is very strong," Perlman says. "My respect for her as an actress is higher than that I have for anyone I've ever worked with. She's terrific, a hard worker, incredibly well disciplined and incredibly respectful of the art and the material, and we get along real well. We find no difficulty in playing those scenes with each other, although we've never talked about it. I guess neither of us want to talk about it, because there's a spirituality between them that remains unspoken between Linda Hamilton and Ron Perlman. We just do it. We don't question it and don't think about it too much. There's that level of trust, which I tip my hat to.

"In terms of the consummation of the relationship," he continues, "we're already getting that question from people. The press hasn't jumped on it yet, but I'm sure they will. I think there's a tremendous amount of heat between these two characters, but whether they take the final step or not, it's there and that's probably what the women who have taken the show and run with it have felt. It's almost not necessary to see it acted out, because it's there in full bloom. Playing that heat within the parameters of what we have to do is an interesting exercise."

A very real concern, naturally, is that what seems fresh and innovative now could turn into cliche as the series continues. This thought has not escaped the actor's attention.

"I'm fearful of that, sure," he admits. "I've been very concerned about the premise of the show, and it's not as if it's falling on deaf ears. Ron Koslow is supervising every single script and every word that goes into every script, and he also knows that this can easily become **The Incredible Hulk** if we're not careful. Using the formula of her getting into trouble, his saving her during the last ten minutes, and the two of them walking off into the sunset is the last thing in the world we want to put in any episode. We're trying to figure out how not to do that; how to make each one almost like a feature film, and I think we've been pretty successful. I think there are times when we've gotten a little bit formula, but I think it's justified—that it follows what has come before in a very organic way.

"In the beginning we were finding our way, and I'll admit there was a bit of formula, but even in the most formula of our scripts, there have always been elements of incredible beauty and abstractness that most other shows don't ever address. Our worst is something that I still think is better than a lot of what you see on TV, and it's the kind of show I've always dreamed of. I really got lucky to find one that is a television series which happens to feel like a movie every week."

While he is confident that the audience for **Beauty and the Beast** will continue, Perlman hopes word of the show will reach the general public.

"If I had the opportunity, I think I'd like to tell people that by tuning into **Beauty and the Beast** they're going to see things they've never seen before, except maybe in motion pictures and on PBS," Perlman closes. "Along with that, I think it's going to be accessible enough, exciting enough and feelingful enough that it's going to drag you in. If this show doesn't drag you in, then you're either cynical, or you don't get it. I just recommend that you give us a try, because once you do, the uniqueness of it is going to overwhelm you. Any show that can end with the Twenty Ninth Sonnet, as one episode did, which airs at 8:00 on network television, can't be all bad."

And the Villain

"The thing that I love about Paracelsus is that he's not just an out-and-out villain, killing people left, right and center with no rhyme, reason or motive," notes actor Tony Jay, perhaps best known as the evil would-be leader of the Underground realm of **Beauty and the Beast**.

"He's a villain with a point of view. Now, maybe you won't agree with that point of view, but at least you'll understand it, and see that he is more than just a two-dimensional character.

"There is a depth to him," he adds, "and a sense of sadness and tragedy about his life. Here is an example of the fantastic tragedy of a man who had the brain and genius to be great, in the best sense of the word, but instead became infamous, which actually happens in our lives. It happened with Hitler, it happened with the Ayatollah Khomeni and it happened with Napoleon. All sorts of infamous people who turned their brilliant minds to the evil side rather than the benign."

Beauty and the Beast, currently preparing for 12 "make-or-break" episodes for mid-season replacement, chronicles the unconsummated love between assistant District Attorney Catherine Chandler (Linda Hamilton), and Vincent (Ron Perlman), the noble lion-man who resides in New York's Underground with hundreds of others who have forsaken the surface world for a life of peace and tranquility. Beyond this relationship, the series has excelled at dealing with poignant human drama, and provided a wide assortment of antagonists, including Paracelsus. Once leader of the Underground, he was exiled by Father (Roy Dotrice) and the rest of the community when his power as an alchemist began corrupting his soul, leading him down a dark path.

Needless to say, this kind of background is particularly gratifying to the Englishman Jay. Unlike most other episodic "guest-villains," he has been given the opportunity to explore his character over the course of six episodes spread throughout the show's first two seasons, thus providing greater depth with each subsequent script.

"As a character goes on, he's bound to change," Jay notes. "Of course when they first write it, they usually don't know who they're writing for, which was the case on **Beauty and the Beast**. Then, when they saw the kind of performance I was delivering, they started to write with me in mind, which is like tailoring the suit to the actor. It's a fusion of their creative work and your interpretation of that work. If they're good writers, which most of them are, they will know whether or not a line rings true in the hands of the actor. So it changes, hopefully for the better. It becomes much more well-oiled, and there are certain mannerisms Paracelsus has that I try to keep, like the occasional little bit of humor and the slightly condescending tone he uses towards Father, because he feels his rightful place is as the head of the Underground. He's been usurped and exiled, and all through it there has been a remembrance and bitterness of that, coupled with this almost sad resignation."

Jay's first appearance on **Beauty and the Beast** was in "The Alchemist," wherein he spreads a self-created powdery narcotic among the surface dwellers, resulting in numerous deaths.

"That was the introduction of Paracelsus, and I really feel it's one of the very best," Jay enthuses. "They did a mystical thing there and introduced us to the enormous kind of invisibility of the character; establishing that he could disappear and come back in other forms. The allusion of the conjurer and magician was there, so that stands out as well as this marvelous ambiance that they managed to get.

"Tom Wright directed that episode, and he is a marvelous director," adds Jay. "He got the best out of it and I remember him saying, 'Less...less...less,' and he got me down to almost the sheer presence of this evil man pervading it, without any histrionics from the theatre. Being a theatre man, I'm inclined to go over the top a little, because it's a very different medium, but he got me down until it was just right. Then, of course, I based everything else on that assumption and they seemed to like it, so I kept with it."

Also interesting about the episode is that it reunited Jay with Roy Dotrice, whom he had worked with in an English stage version of ***Great Expectations*** and with whom he has remained friends ever since.

"In 'The Alchemist' there was that wonderful scene where Roy tells me that I have to stop selling this dust because it's killing people," Jay recalls, "and we had that terrific confrontation, which Ron Koslow called the best scene ever on **Beauty and the Beast**. So working with someone like Roy, especially being great friends with him, helps a great deal. He's on your side and you're working off of, and giving to, each other. It's the same on stage, because if you've got a friend on stage, you know he's not going to try silly things. He's going to trust you and you're going to trust them."

He followed with "To Reign in Hell," in which Paracelsus kidnaps Catherine and brings her to the bowels of the Underground. Vincent, in a series of events akin to J.R.R. Tolkien's ***The Lord of the Rings***, puts together a fellowship whose mission is to find her.

"That showed Parcelsus as a man of learning, because he quotes Milton: 'It is better to reign in Hell than to serve in Heaven.' That shows he was a learned man and also gave us some samples of his quirky humor," Jay says. "He was very amused by things. That was nice and very good, compounding his threat and the menace when he steals Cathy. The nice thing is that Paracelsus escapes once more."

In "The Dead of Winter," the Underground is preparing for its annual Winterfest, which Paracelsus disrupts in his usual fashion.

"Personally, after 'The Alchemist' this is my favorite," Jay states. "I liked the whole feeling of joy and this pervading sense of menace over it all when they find out that Paracelsus is among them, disguised as somebody. It turned out to be Lou the barber, and it presented the first signs of his power to impersonate other people."

In "Remember Love," an angel shows Vincent what life for Catherine and the Underground would be like if he did not exist. In this parallel world, Parcelsus remained ruler and dictator.

"I wasn't too struck with that one," Jay admits. "I thought it had too many uncomfortable allusions to **It's a Wonderful Life**."

Perhaps his most dramatic appearance came in two out of three episodes of a "trilogy" presented at season two's end, in which Vincent must confront the beast within him, and Parcelsus provides considerable information pertaining to both his and Vincent's backgrounds, although the validity of these revelations remain to be seen.

"In 'What Rough Beast' Parcelsus masqueraded as Elliot Birch, and was telling a reporter all about Vincent and the Underground to expose them," Jay explains. "I particularly liked that small scene with the reporter where he dies that terrible death at Parcelsus' blade. It was totally unexpected, I thought, but it all made sense. The script was beautifully thought out, and it was nice to have Paracelsus in everyday clothes for a change.

"My final show was 'In A Ceremony of Innocense,' where he masquerades as Father. I'm not decided on that one, because one doesn't quite know whether Paracelsus is dead or not. If he is dead, will he come back? Has he been fatally wounded, or what? Nobody really mentions it, so I think they deliberately did it that way so that there would be room to bring him back, if that's the way they see it."

The finest moment of the latter episode is when Paracelsus, disguised as Father, verbally assaults Vincent, forcing him to confront the evil in his own soul and goading him on until the beast unleashes an apparent deathblow.

"Roy did that scene brilliantly," Jay says with admiration. "He was unlike Father, which is what gave Vincent the clue that this might not be Father talking to him. On the other hand, I can't be sure if he realized it, but when Paracelsus as Father goads him into a final attack, we find out that he was Vincent's actual father.

"It was a little vague, and I think they deliberately did that. Apparently, as far as I can see, he had a wife called Anna, and they couldn't have children because he was impotent. Then he started conducting experiments to give her a baby—some kind of seminal implant—and of course that went hideously wrong, and produced Vincent. As far as Parcelsus' story is concerned, that's what we're stuck with. For some reason or another, they've left that open. We don't know what that reason is yet. It wasn't totally clear, but a lot of questions were answered. Whether or not it's the truth is another matter."

One truth that cannot be avoided is that Tony Jay, at age 56, has become one of Hollywood's newest faces. His career actually began at the age of

32, when he decided to leave a very successful real estate business behind him to pursue his thespian aspirations.

"I was always an actor at school, but when I came out of the Royal Air Force at the age of 20, I decided I would go with a much more safe, secure and financially remunerative occupation," he says regarding his real estate venture. "So I tried to ignore acting, keeping my hand in amateur work. Then things became very strange."

Jay and his first wife moved to South Africa with the understanding that real estate was "terrific" there, but within three months he found himself acting on radio. A strong believer in "divine force," he felt that his destiny had become vivid, and that acting was the direction he should go in.

"I did radio for seven years and some film," he recalls, "but when I returned to London at the age of 40, I was totally unknown. Of course I had never acted professionally in my own country, so I had to start all over again."

While in England over the next 14 years, he appeared in a variety of television and stage productions. In terms of the former, he was featured in a television series entitled **The Fall of Eagles**, which happened to co-star the newest captain of the starship Enterprise, Patrick Stewart.

"The show was about the fall of the Romanovs in Russia. I played Czar Alexander III, and Patrick played Lenin. We met then and at odd times here and there, then we lost touch totally. I was startled and very pleased to find out that he was doing **Star Trek**. Patrick would know who I am, because the British acting profession is very small, actually."

As far as stage is concerned, his credits include Peter Ustinov's :The Unknown Soldier and His Wife," "The Deep Blue Sea," "The Merchant of Venice" and "A View From the Bridge." Interestingly, during this time he was the first person offered a key role in George Lucas' **Star Wars**.

"If it weren't for Alec Guiness," he says without regret, "I would have had the role of Obi Wan Kenobi in **Star Wars**, which was called 'Galactic Warfare' at the time. I was the first one to be interviewed for that role. Lucas came over, I was asked to go meet him at 20th Century Fox and I didn't even know who he was. He had just done **American Graffiti**, but I had never seen the film. He said, 'We're doing this science fiction movie, Mr. Jay, and you're exactly right for this role. We don't want any stars, because we're putting the money into the effects. I want you to meet my partner in three month's time. We're doing the movie at Pinewood Studios,' and so on. I said, 'Alright,' but it really didn't matter. Who knew what it was going to be? The next thing I know, it was Alec Guiness and I never heard from Lucas again. When you think about it, he had Harrison Ford, Mark Hamill and Carrie Fisher, all of whom were totally unknown. I think he got cold feet and decided that he had to have some kind of star. Who knows what I would be doing today if I had been Obi Wan Kenobi?"

Fame of a different kind greeted him when he was asked to co-star in the Royal Shakespeare Company's version of ***Nicholas Nickleby***. Not only was the show, which toured the UK and played in Los Angeles and New York, a huge success, but it opened the door for him to begin his American acting career.

"As a result of the show," Jay explains, "I was approached by the agent, Harry Abrahms, but I told him it was hopeless, because first of all, I had a nice career in England and, second, I didn't know anyone in America and it's extremely difficult to get into the states. It's almost impossible, unless you have a sponsor. He said, 'We'll see what we can do.' So I went back home, and three months later Phoenix Entertainment, who had seen 'Nicholas Nickleby,' asked me to test for the lead in a pilot called **Circus**, and they brought me back to America to test. We did the pilot, it didn't get picked up, but I met my wife, who was the make-up artist, on the set, and I eventually married her and became a resident, although that's not the reason I married her. Now we've got a six month old son. It just seems kind of destined. I've been here now for over two years, but really only seriously involved in work over the last eighteen or nineteen months."

He began his American acting career on episodic television in such series as **Hunter**, **Golden Girls**, **Beverly Hills Buntz**, **Supercarrier** and, of course, **Beauty and the Beast**, and was featured in the films **Twins** and **My Stepmother Is an Alien**. One thing he is particularly grateful for is the opportunity that America has given him in terms of versatility.

"In England we look upon what I've done there as par for the course," Jay laughs in a voice that is far more gentle in tone than that of Parcelsus, "and they're worried about versatility. If they can't put you into a pigeon hole, they get very worried, and I think the same applies here, to a certain extent. But in England I had to struggle to avoid playing the same things again and again, such as doctors, lawyers and professors. Here I've had no problem. On **Hunter** I played an Irish priest. On **Golden Girls** I was a Hungarian sculptor, on **Beverly Hills Buntz** I was an Arab sheik, in **Supercarrier** I played a French professor and Parcelsus is kind of a dramatic role in the theatrical sense. In **Twins** I played a German father; a kindly professor. **In My Stepmother is an Alien**, I played a chief counsel in space, where you see me 40 feet high on a hologram, and director Richard Benjamin wanted me to play it very English. My portrayals have been all over the place, and I like it like that. There are some people who are afraid of versatility, but I embrace it."

While he is generally pleased with the final product of **My Stepmother is an Alien**, Jay is mystified by the film's lack of boxoffice success and can offer no reasonable explanation. By the same token, he is curious as to the success of the Arnold Schwarzenegger-Danny DeVito vehicle, **Twins**, in which one of his key scenes as Schwarzenegger's kindly father figure/ professor was left on the cutting room floor.

"I had a minute or two more on screen," he says, "but because we didn't get to Danny DeVito and Arnold quick enough, they cut me. I had a very big fight with director Ivan Reitman over that, because it was a very revelatory scene that they cut. It explained why we were doing such dreadful things, and why I was against the wicked doctor. We explained all that, but they just cut it out and I feel it was wrong. Not because it was me, but because it was an important scene that explained alot. But there you are, they just threw it out. They think the film holds together without an explanation, and it doesn't. But what do I know? They made over a hundred million dollars in this country. Go argue with city hall, right? If money at the box office is the whole criteria, **Twins** has got to be a great film. Of course it's not a great film, although it could have been if they weren't thinking of only the commercial angle."

Although he doesn't come right out and say it, it's obvious from the way he speaks that it is Paracelsus and **Beauty and the Beast** that rank highest on Jay's list of his credentials, and he is particularly intrigued by the suggestion that his character represents Vincent's dark side.

"Yes, it almost seems that way, doesn't it?" he asks rhetorically. "Of course Parcelsus' own philosophy about evil is that you must own up to it and claim it as part of your glory, as he said to Vincent. He feels that the Underground people underestimate him, and therefore don't let him be his own natural self. He's an animal, and here's Cathy bringing out the romantic, tender and noble sides. The master stroke, of course, was having Vincent be a lion, because the lion is a noble animal and the king of the jungle. Although he's a beast, he has a wonderful side of sensitivity and another side of primeval violence, which animals have. It's in the best tradition of mythology and the great medieval stories. It's lovely seeing it today, given a 1989 slant.

"**Beauty and the Beast** has been done before," he continues. "All Ron Koslow did, which was very clever of him, was set it in modern times, seeing what happens when an assistant DA, a beautiful woman, meets the beast in the Underground tunnels. It's a marvelous idea, and I suppose if it disappears off the screen, at least we'll be grateful for having two seasons. It could be the sort of thing that's ahead of its time, and one that will gain a cult following later on, although there's a strong cult following now."

Surprisingly, **Beauty and the Beast** had a highly successful first season, but a disastrous year two. Viewers began to tune out. Jay has his own—highly personal, he emphasizes—opinion as to what happened.

"I believe there was a number of things," he opines. "I think they just lost that sense of antagonism. You must have conflict in everything that you do, whether you're writing a piece of music, a play or even painting a picture. It's hard for me to talk about that where **Beauty and the Beast** is concerned, because there can be a number of reasons as to why it lost viewers. The Writer's Guild strike certainly didn't help. It made them late, and they didn't get the foothold they wanted early in the season. Also, I would say that it had just a little too much of the romantic, whispering poetry. If you put it in little doses here and there, but broke it up with action scenes, then that would have been the right recipe. But to be fair to them, I think they were misled by the viewers who loved, at the beginning, the idea of the love interest between beauty and the beast. Of course you can't consummate that kind of relationship on CBS network television, so where can you go with it? Unfortunately I think—and this is my personal opinion—they took that love interest too far, and too long, and I think people had a sense of sameness every week."

At the time of writing, the series is struggling to remain on the air. As stated at the outset, CBS had ordered 12 final episodes for mid-season replacement, and their subsequent ratings will determine whether or not the show returns for a fourth year. At the time of reading, you may know the answer. While Jay has no information concerning the direction of those 12 shows, he has heard that Paracelsus might return, despite the character being killed by Vincent.

"If they can bring Patrick Duffy back on Dallas, they can certainly bring back Paracelsus," he laughs. "They've brought back many characters on TV shows, even though that character was supposed to be dead. Remember, Paracelsus has died before. There have been other times where he's disappeared without a trace and come back, but this time, I do admit, they've made quite a point of the death. I still think he's inhuman, and as an inhuman he can do anything. He's an alchemist. He's a magician. He's a wizard. He's that old fable running back through the centuries to Medieval times.

"If Parcelsus is brought back, and it is a big if, then I would say I would like to see him, as you quite rightly put it, as the alter-ego of Vincent; symbolizing what Vincent could have become had it not been for the tender graces of his other side and the effect that Cathy and Father have had on him." Jay, who will show up next in an episode of the syndicated **Lassie**, closes, "They are influences of the good, where Paracelsus provides influences of the bad. I'd like to see that and his background developed a little bit more. What was he in his earlier days? How did he get involved in all this? What exactly happened? There's a certain amount of scope for that, but above all else, he should always remain evil, but evil with a point of view. There should always be a reason for his evil."

Season 2 - Taped

1. Brothers
2. The Outsiders
3. Arabesque
4. Sticks and Stones
5. When the Bluebird Sings
6. The ~~Peeping Tom~~ Watcher
7. A Distant Shore
8. Ashes, Ashes
9. Dead of Winter
10. A Fair and Perfect Knight
11. Orphans
12. Trial
13. A Kingdom By the Sea
14. The Hollow Men
15. God Bless the Child
16. Labyrinths
17. A Gentle Rain
18. Ceremony of Innocence
19. The Rest Is Silence

The World's Only Official

COUCH POTATO BOOK CATALOG™

Please note:
You must be a certified couch potato* to partake of this offering!

* To become a certified couch potato you must watch a minimum of 25 hours a day at least 8 days per week.

From Happy Hal...

Star Trek
Gunsmoke
The Man from U.N.C.L.E.

They all evoke golden memories of lost days of decades past. What were you doing when you first saw them?

Were you sitting with your parents and brothers and sisters gathered around a small set in your living room?

Were you in your own apartment just setting out on the wonders of supporting yourself, with all of the many associated fears?

Or were you off at some golden summer camp with all of the associated memories, of course forgetting the plague of mosquitoes and the long, arduous hikes?

The memories of the television show are mixed with the memories of the time in a magical blend that always brings a smile to your face. Hopefully we can help bring some of the smiles to life, lighting up your eyes and heart with our work...

Look inside at the **UNCLE Technical Manual**, the **Star Trek Encyclopedia, The Compleat Lost in Space** or the many, many other books about your favorite television shows!

Let me know what you think of our books.

And what you want to see.

It's the only way we can share our love of the wonders of the magic box....

Selection

HAL SCHUSTER

Administration

JACK SCHUSTER,
COUCH POTATO

Customer Service

PHYLLIS SCHUSTER

All correspondence:
5715 N. Balsam Rd.
Las Vegas, NV 89130

From The Couch Potato...

I am here working hard on your orders.

Let me tell you about a few new things we have added to help speed up your order. First we are computerizing the way we process your order so that we can more easily look it up if we need to and maintain our customer list. The program will also help us process our shipping information by including weight, location and ordering information which will be essential if you have a question or complaint (Heavens Forbid).

We are now using UPS more than the post office. This helps in many ways including tracing a package if it is lost and in more speedily getting your package to you because they are quicker. . They are also more careful with shipments and they arrive in better condition. UPS costs a little more than post office, This is unfortunate but we feel you will find that it is worth it.

Also please note our new discount program. Discounts range from 5% to 20% off.

So things are looking up in 1988 for Coach Potato.

I really appreciate your orders and time but I really must get back to the tube...

SPIES SPIES SPIES SPI

THE COUCH POTATO BOOK CATALOG 5715 N BALSAM, LAS VEGAS, NV 89130

The Phantom
The Green Hornet
The Shadow
The Batman

Each issue of Serials Adventures Presents offers 100 or more pages of pure nostalgic fun for $16.95

Flash Gordon Part One
Flash Gordon Part Two
Blackhawk

Each issue of Serials Adventures Presents features a chapter by chapter review of a rare serial combined with biographies of the stars and behind-the-scenes information. Plus rare photos. See the videotapes and read the books!

UNCLE

THE U.N.C.L.E. TECHNICAL MANUAL

Every technical device completely detailed and blueprinted, including weapons, communications, weaponry, organization, facitilites... 80 pages, 2 volumes...$9.95 each

PRISONER

NUMBER SIX: THE COMPLEAT PRISONER

The most unique and intelligent television series ever aired! Patrick McGoohan's tour-de-force of spies and mental mazes finally explained episode by episode, including an interview with the McGoohan and the complete layout of the real village!...160 pages...$14.95

GREEN HORNET TELEVISION

THE GREEN HORNET

Daring action adventure with the Green Hornet and Kato. This show appeared before Bruce Lee had achieved popularity but delivered fun, superheroic action. Episode guide and character profiles combine to tell the whole story...120 pages...$14.95

WILD, WILD WEST

WILD, WILD, WEST

Is it a Western or a Spy show? We couldn't decide so we're listing it twice. Fantastic adventure, convoluted plots, incredible devices...all set in the wild, wild west! Details of fantastic devices, character profiles and an episode-by-episode guide...120 pages...$17.95

THE COUCH POTATO BOOK CATALOG 5715 N BALSAM, LAS VEGAS, NV 89130

SPIES SPIES SPIES SPI

THE ILLUSTRATED STEPHEN KING
A complee guide to the novels and short stories of Stephen King illustrated by Steve Bissette and others...$12.95

GUNSMOKE YEARS
The definitive book of America's most successful television series. 22 years of episode guide, character profiles, interviews and more...240 pages, $14.95

THE KING COMIC HEROES
The complete story of the King Features heroes including Prince Valiant, Flash Gordon, Mandrake, The Phantom, Secret Agent, Rip Kirby, Buz Sawyer, Johnny Hazard and Jungle Jim. These fabulous heroes not only appeared in comic strips and comic books but also in movies and serials, Includes interviews with Hal Foster, Al Williamson and Lee Falk...$14.95

Special discounts are available for library, school, club or other bulk orders. Please inquire.

**IF YOUR FAVORITE TELEVISION SERIES ISN'T HERE, LET US KNOW...
AND THEN STAY TUNED!**

And always remember that if every world leader was a couch potato and watched TV 25 hours a day, 8 days a week, there would be no war...

Boring, but Necessary Ordering Information!

Payment: All orders must be prepaid by check or money order. Do not send cash. All payments must be made in US funds only.

Shipping: We offer several methods of shipment for our product.

Postage is as follows:

For books priced under $10.00— for the first book add $2.50. For each additional book under $10.00 add $1.00. (This is per individual book priced under $10.00, not the order total.)

For books priced over $10.00— for the first book add $3.25. For each additional book over $10.00 add $2.00. (This is per individual book priced over $10.00, not the order total.)

These orders are filled as quickly as possible. Sometimes a book can be delayed if we are temporarily out of stock. You should note on your order whether you prefer us to ship the book as soon as available or send you a merchandise credit good for other TV goodies or send you your money back immediately. Shipments normally take 2 or 3 weeks, but allow up to12 weeks for delivery.

Special UPS 2 Day Blue Label RUSH SERVICE: Special service is available for desperate Couch Potatos. These books are shipped within 24 hours of when we receive your order and should take 2 days to get from us to you.

For the first **RUSH SERVICE** book under $10.00 add $4.00. For each additional 1 book under $10.00 and $1.25. (This is per individual book priced under $10.00, not the order total.)

For the first **RUSH SERVICE** book over $10.00 add $6.00. For each additional book over $10.00 add $3.50 per book. (This is per individual book priced over $10.00, not the order total.)

Canadian and Foreign shipping rates are the same except that Blue Label RUSH SERVICE is not available. All Canadian and Foreign orders are shipped as books or printed matter.

DISCOUNTS! DISCOUNTS! Because your orders are what keep us in business we offer a discount to people that buy a lot of our books as our way of saying thanks. On orders over $25.00 we give a 5% discount. On orders over $50.00 we give a 10% discount. On orders over $100.00 we give a 15% discount. On orders over $150.00 we give a 20% discount. Please list alternates when possible. Please state if you wish a refund or for us to backorder an item if it is not in stock.

100% satisfaction guaranteed. We value your support. You will receive a full refund as long as the copy of the book you are not happy with is received back by us in reasonable condition. No questions asked, except we would like to know how we failed you. Refunds and credits are given as soon as we receive back the item you do not want.

Please have mercy on Phyllis and carefully fill out this form in the neatest way you can. Remember, she has to read a lot of them every day and she wants to get it right and keep you happy! You may use a duplicate of this order blank as long as it is clear. **Please don't forget to include payment! And remember, we *love* repeat friends...**

ORDER FORM

_____The Phantom $16.95
_____The Green Hornet $16.95
_____The Shadow $16.95
_____Flash Gordon Part One $16.95_____Part Two $16.95
_____Blackhawk $16.95
_____Batman $16.95
_____The UNCLE Technical Manual One $9.95 _____Two $9.95
_____The Green Hornet Television Book $14.95
_____Number Six The Prisoner Book $14.95
_____The Wild Wild West $17.95
_____Trek Year One $10.95
_____Trek Year Two $12.95
_____Trek Year Three $12.95
_____The Animated Trek $14.95
_____The Movies $12.95
_____Next Generation $19.95
_____The Lost Years $14.95
_____The Trek Encyclopedia $19.95
_____Interviews Aboard The Enterprise $18.95
_____The Ultimate Trek $75.00
_____Trek Handbook $12.95_____Trek Universe $17.95
_____The Crew Book $17.95
_____The Making of the Next Generation $14.95
_____The Freddy Krueger Story $14.95
_____The Aliens Story $14.95
_____Robocop $16.95
_____Monsterland's Horror in the '80s $17.95
_____The Compleat Lost in Space $17.95
_____Lost in Space Tribute Book $9.95
_____Lost in Space Tech Manual $9.95
_____Supermarionation $17.95
_____The Unofficial Beauty and the Beast $14.95
_____Dark Shadows Tribute Book $14.95
_____Dark Shadows Interview Book $18.95
_____Doctor Who Baker Years $19.95
_____The Doctor Who Encyclopedia:The 4th Doctor $19.95
_____Illustrated Stephen King $12.95
_____Gunsmoke Years $14.95

NAME:_______________

STREET:_______________

CITY:_______________

STATE:_______________

ZIP:_______________

TOTAL:__________ SHIPPING__________

**SEND TO: COUCH POTATO,INC.
5715 N BALSAM, LAS VEGAS, NV 89130**